Romans
Volume I: Saved by Faith

Romans 1:1–5:21
by Theodore H. Epp
Director
Back to the Bible Broadcast

A
**BACK TO THE BIBLE
PUBLICATION**

A Do-It-Yourself Course

12 units

published by

Back to the Bible Correspondence School
Lincoln, Nebraska 68501

78,000 printed to date—1976
(5-5901—75M—126)
ISBN 0-8474-2306-9

Printed in the United States of America

Instructions

Please read these instructions before beginning the study of your lessons.

The Reason for Study

As you enter into the study of God's Word, remember that you are studying the greatest book ever written, because it is inspired by God Himself. Its message has a unique power. If believed and obeyed, it changes a life not only for time but also for eternity. Men have suffered and died that we might have the Bible in our own language. So, let us not neglect it, but let us study it diligently that we might be "approved unto God," workmen who need not be ashamed, rightly dividing the word of truth (II Tim. 2:15).

Your study of God's Word should not be merely for accumulating facts but for obtaining a personal understanding of who God is and what He wants to accomplish through your life.

Suggestions for Study

Preparation for Study

If at all possible, find a place where there are no distractions. This will make it easier to concentrate. If you have particular difficulty in concentrating, you may find it helpful to read the study material aloud.

Pray for God's help. Before studying each lesson, ask God to show you the significance of the truths you are about to consider. Ask God, the author of the Scriptures, to teach you more about Himself and His holy Word.

Materials for Study

A Bible. This is your main textbook. This course is designed to help you know your Bible better. The final authority is not the course but the Word of God, upon which this course is based.

A dictionary. Use a dictionary whenever necessary to find the meaning of words you do not understand.

A pencil, pen or marker. Use this tool to underscore important words or phrases. As you scan through the course later, the underlined words will help you to recall quickly the thought of each unit.

Method of Study

Begin your actual study by reading the first unit in this course. You may find it helpful to read the entire lesson quickly, taking special note of the main headings. Then read it again, making a more detailed study of the unit. During your second reading, be sure to look up each Scripture reference. Study the unit until you have mastered it.

Begin work on your new memory assignment when you start a new unit. Go over your memory verses several times each day, repeating the reference before and after each verse. This will help you to remember its location.

Think over the teaching of the unit, and apply the truths to your life. Ask the Lord to show you how you can use these principles to help you in living for Him.

Turn to the examination, which is on the last two pages of the unit. Do not take the examination yet, but look over the questions to determine what areas you need to study further. Then look for the answers in the unit or in your Bible.

How to Take the Examinations

After you have studied Unit 1 and reviewed it carefully, take the examination without referring to your textbook or any notes you may have taken. Where Scripture references are given in the question, you may use your Bible to refer to the passages, except where direct quotations are required to be written in the blanks. Memory work can be checked by reciting the verses to someone or by writing them out on a separate piece of paper and then checking them with the Bible.

After you have completed the examination, check your answers with those in the Answer Key, which begins on page 100. When answers do not agree, carefully review the part of the lesson involved and the related Bible verses. Follow the same procedure with other units.

Plan Your Study

You are the best judge of how much time to allow for each unit. We recommend, however, that you plan to complete one unit each week. Regular study is best. But don't worry if it takes longer than we suggest. Remember, you are studying God's Word, and you are wisely investing your time.

Do not send the examinations for this Do-It-Yourself Course to us for grading, but keep them in this book. If you have questions concerning this course and have no one to help you, you may write to us at Back to the Bible Correspondence School, Box 82808, Lincoln, Nebraska 68501. We also stand ready to help you with any spiritual problem you may wish to share with us.

Contents

BACK TO THE BIBLE BROADCAST

THE GOOD NEWS BROADCASTING ASSOCIATION, INC.
BOX 82808 • LINCOLN, NEBRASKA 68501
TELEPHONE 402/435-2171

THEODORE H. EPP, DIRECTOR
MELVIN A. JONES, EXEC. DIRECTOR

Dear Student:

One of the best ways to study the Bible is to concentrate on an entire book. While the topical method of Bible study is the simplest, we must study the Word of God book by book in order to see the complete picture of the Person and work of Jesus Christ. This is one reason why I am so glad that you enrolled in this course.

The Christian is called to bear fruit. If there is to be fruit, seed must be sown and the seed is the Word of God. First of all, the Word must find its way into the hearts of men. Only as we meditate upon the Word of God can we obtain power for everyday Christian living.

"But his delight is in the law of the Lord; and in his law doth he meditate day and night. And he shall be like a tree planted by the rivers of water, that bringeth forth his fruit in his season; his leaf also shall not wither; and whatsoever he doeth shall prosper" (Ps. 1:2,3). Please note that all-inclusive promise--"Whatsoever he doeth shall prosper."

We are praying for you as you study this course. God bless you.

Yours in Him,

Theo. H. Epp

Theodore H. Epp

unit 1

The Message of Romans

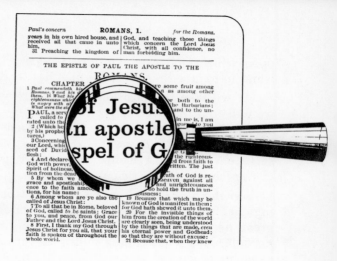

One name stands out above all others in the Book of Romans. It is the name "Jesus." The Apostle Paul described himself as "a servant of Jesus Christ, called to be an apostle, separated unto the gospel of God . . . Concerning his son Jesus Christ our Lord, which was made of the seed of David according to the flesh; And declared to be the Son of God with power, according to the spirit of holiness, by the resurrection from the dead" (1:1-4). As we see here, this name is usually coupled with others such as "Jesus Christ"; "His Son, Jesus Christ our Lord"; "Son of God"; and "the Lord Jesus Christ."

The name "Jesus" is generally thought of as being His earthly name. The word "Christ" means "the anointed One, the Messiah." The word "Lord" speaks to us of His administration of the universe, of His work in the lives of His people today, and of His ruling as King throughout all eternity.

God's redemption is through Jesus Christ. The Scripture just quoted shows us that God sent His Son, who is eternally God, into the world that He might become as a man, humble Himself, and die the shameful death of the cross.

Grace

This now brings us to the word "grace," for by Jesus "we have received grace." To many people, grace is some sort of blessing that they are unable to define. In reality, it is an attribute of God. It is that part of God which governs His attitude toward man. It is in the heart of God to want to do something for someone who is in need. Man is born with a need,

9

upon which God can exercise His grace. Grace, then, is God's wanting to give to man that which he stands in need of.

If we take the position that we are worthy of God's grace, we will find that we really are not. If any one of us would come before God and say, "I have lived a good life, Lord, and have a good character, and would, therefore, like to have your all-sufficient grace," it would be refused us. God cannot shower His grace on self-sufficient persons.

On the other hand, when we stand before God acknowledging that we are sinners and justly condemned, and feeling our great need, then God's grace will be released to supply that need. This is what God is telling us through Paul. Jesus Christ came in grace to save condemned sinners. He loved us while we were sinners and died for us while we were His enemies.

The Power of the Gospel

The Apostle Paul stated the theme of the Book of Romans in these words: "I am not ashamed of the gospel of Christ: for it is the power of God unto salvation to every one that believeth; to the Jew first, and also to the Greek" (1:16). Just how much the word "salvation" includes will be seen as the theme is developed. Far more than removal of guilt is meant. It is no wonder that Paul, in having come to a full comprehension of the gospel, declared, "I am not ashamed of the gospel of Christ."

Paul knew that the gospel was not some inferior thing. Neither was it untried, for it had been put to the test, and never once had it resulted in a failure. The gospel is not one of several remedies for the sin question, all of which might work. It cannot be classified as part of a creed or a mere dogma.

Paul says that here is something that is a proven fact— something that is real. It is good news for which he had no reason to be ashamed. It is good news concerning Christ, and Christ is God. The Scriptures say of Christ that He "is the image of the invisible God, the firstborn of every creature" (Col. 1:15). This verse tells us that Christ existed before any created thing; in fact, He always was. The passage continues: "For by him were all things created, that are in heaven, and that are in earth, visible and invisible, whether they be thrones, or dominions, or principalities, or powers: all things were created by him, and for him: And he is before all things, and by him all things consist" (vv. 16,17).

The gospel concerns this Person. With such a Person as Christ to present, it is no wonder Paul was not ashamed. And for the same reason we do not need to be ashamed. We read in the Scriptures that Christ made the worlds and He upholds all things by the Word of His power. Ashamed of Him? Surely not!

The gospel of Christ is the demonstration of the power of God unto salvation. This is something man is desperately in need of. By nature we all come into this world spiritually dead to God.

Spiritual Death Through Adam

Consider our first parents—Adam and Eve. They were created in the image of God and the spirit of life was in them. In the second chapter of Genesis we learn that they were warned of judgment if they disobeyed God with reference to the tree of the knowledge of good and evil. They were told that the day they ate of its fruit they would die. Death in this case, was not only physical death, but spiritual death—separation from God.

Adam and Eve did not heed God. The third chapter of Genesis tells the sad story of the Fall. They disobeyed God and immediately died spiritually. Physical death followed at a later time.

In dying to God, Adam brought the whole race into death with him. A number of Scriptures point this out. One of these is Romans 5:12 where Paul says, "Wherefore, as by one man sin entered into the world, and death by sin; and so death passed upon all men, for that all have sinned." Agreeing with this is I Corinthians 15:22: "For as in Adam all die." Paul expresses this truth in another way in Ephesians where he writes: "Being alienated from the life of God through the ignorance that is in them, because of the blindness of their heart" (Eph. 4:18). This was our condition before we met Christ.

If a person rejects Christ he will ultimately be separated from God eternally. This is known as the second death. Of this the Apostle John wrote in the Book of the Revelation: "And death and hell were cast into the lake of fire. This is the second death" (20:14). Again we read in Revelation 21:8: "But the fearful, and unbelieving, and the abominable, and murderers, and whoremongers, and sorcerers, and idolaters, and all liars, shall have their part in the lake which burneth with fire and brimstone: which is the second death." Such is the destiny of all who in this life reject God's offer of salvation through Christ.

Life Only Through Christ

If we are not born again, then all we have is our birth in Adam which leaves us void of all spiritual life. The remedy to this condition calls for a power greater than man can produce. It calls for something that can produce life. Religion, as such, may tell us how to act under certain conditions, but it can never give us spiritual life. This comes only from God, and He gives it only through Christ. "In him was life" (John 1:4). He came that we might have life. Yet, so reluctant were men to receive this life that the Lord Jesus said to some of them, "Ye will not come to me that ye might have life." Nevertheless, His offer is still extended: "He that heareth my word, and believeth on him that sent me, hath everlasting life, and shall not come into condemnation; but is passed from death unto life" (John 5:24).

This gospel of which Paul was not ashamed is the Good News that God through Christ produces life in those who are spiritually dead. There is no cause for shame in a gospel like this. Spiritual life is made available through Christ to all who will trust in Him, that is, to all who believe. To as many as received Him He gives the power to become the sons of God (John 1:12). All who come unto Christ pass from death to life. Furthermore, all who come to Him, He will in no wise cast out (John 6:37).

Salvation by Blood

There was a time when Israel was hopelessly enslaved in Egypt. There was no chance, humanly speaking, for them ever to gain their freedom. But God intervened. He came and demonstrated His power. He brought judgment upon Egypt which is a type of the world, but at the same time He provided a way of escape for the Israelites. They were saved from the judgment that fell upon Egypt. Chapter 12 of Exodus records the history of that time. The blood of a lamb had to be applied to the doorposts and lintel. God's promise was that on the night when the death angel was to pass over Egypt, those houses marked by the blood would find their firstborn protected. God said, "When I see the blood, I will pass over you."

There is a great deal of religion today, but it is bloodless religion. The followers of such religions may be fine people, but when they leave out the blood they are following Satan who is trying to deceive us. Satan hates the blood because it is through the blood of Christ that he, Satan, was conquered. The Bible is very explicit in stating, "without the shedding of blood, there is no remission of sin." An essential part of the Good News is that God not only sent His Son into this world, but that the Son also died—shed His blood—for the sins of men.

Salvation by Power

To be saved from the guilt and consequences of sin is not all of the Good News, however. The gospel we are told here in Romans 1:16 is "the power of God." Too many of God's people have been satisfied with the forgiveness of sins and with that alone. But such does not please God, because through the new birth He has implanted a new life within us which is Christ in us, our "hope of glory."

Let us see how this worked out in the experience of Israel which has been recorded for our benefit. Israel was saved first of all from the judgment that fell on Egypt by blood. Then she was saved from the enslavement of Egypt by God's power at the Red Sea. A tremendous miracle was wrought when God opened up those waters so that His people could pass safely to the other side.

God's assurance to His ancient people was, "Fear ye not, stand still, and see the salvation of the Lord, which he will shew to you to day: for the Egyptians whom ye have seen to day, ye shall see them again no more for ever. The Lord shall fight for you, and ye shall hold your peace" (Ex. 14:13,14). God pushed the waters back and the Israelites marched through the sea and were thereby delivered from the Egyptian army.

The lesson for us is that God not only saves us from the guilt of sin, but also from the power of sin. Salvation is by blood and by power. It is a complete salvation. This is the gospel, the Good News in Christ.

Imputed Righteousness

We still have not exhausted the content of the Good News of salvation in Christ, for verse 17 of Romans 1 carries us on to another truth. It reads, "For therein [the gospel] is the righteousness of God revealed from faith to faith: as it is written, The just shall live by faith." The gospel revealed God's plan for imputing righteousness. We are not only saved from condemnation of sin, and from the power of sin, but we are given a standing in righteousness before God. Our own righteous acts could never produce this right standing before God. We need a righteousness before Him that is identical to Christ's righteousness.

God does not tell us to try to work up this righteousness because, as we have already seen, our good works could not produce it. The fact remains, however, that without this righteousness we can never stand in God's presence. It is here that we see another aspect of this glorious gospel. It reveals God's righteousness—a righteousness which God puts on our account. This is God's great plan of bringing man back into right standing with Himself. It is of this that He speaks in Romans 3:21,22 where we read: "But now the righteousness of God without the law is manifested, being witnessed by the law and the prophets; Even the righteousness of God which is by faith of Jesus Christ unto all and upon all them that believe: for there is no difference"; Or again in verse 26 of the same chapter: "To declare, I say, at this time his righteousness: that he might be just, and the justifier of him which believeth in Jesus."

This means that God is going to put the righteousness of Jesus on our account. He reckons the righteousness of Christ to be our righteousness. Yes, more than that, Christ himself has become our righteousness. It is this that puts us in right standing with God. So then, when we come before God, united with Christ, we have the only kind of standing before God that He will recognize.

God must put away sin. He is righteous in His character and cannot overlook sin. He cannot tolerate evil; so to be just, He put away sin by the death of Jesus Christ. But to justify us —to give us a right standing before Himself, He took the righteousness of Jesus and put it on our account. He put our sins on

Jesus' account and put Jesus' righteousness on our account. God made Christ to be sin for us, then Christ became our righteousness.

Memory Assignment:
Memorize Romans 1:16.

EXAMINATION

Complete the following:

1. The name _____ is generally considered the earthly name for the Son of God.

2. The name _____ means "the Anointed One, the Messiah."

3. The name _____ refers to the Son of God as controller of men's lives and of the universe.

4. The desire of God to give man that which he needs is called God's _____.

5. Paul said, "I am not ashamed of the gospel of Christ: for it is the _____ of _____ unto _____ to every one that believeth."

In the blank space at the right-hand margin write the letter of the correct or most nearly correct answer.

6. By nature we all come into this world:
   (a) as children of God
   (b) with a spark of divine life
   (c) spiritually dead to God   _____

7. In Genesis 2 God told Adam and Eve that eating from the tree of knowledge of good and evil would:
   (a) make them as gods, knowing good and evil
   (b) bring them death
   (c) bring them eternal life   _____

8. Religion in itself can provide:
   (a) spiritual life
   (b) a guide for proper actions
   (c) peace of heart   _____

9. God's requirement for the remission of sin is:
   (a) obedience
   (b) repentance
   (c) the shedding of blood   _____

10. The account of God's miraculous deliverance of Israel through the Red Sea reminds us that:
    (a) God's power is an important part of our salvation
    (b) God's power alone has accomplished our salvation
    (c) God saves us only from the power of sin   _____

In the right-hand margin write "True" or "False" after each of the following statements:

11. Salvation can be summarized as deliverance from the guilt and consequences of sin.   _____

12. A conscientious person by carefully living up to God's standards can attain the righteousness which God requires for salvation.   _____

13. A right standing with God is determined by the kind of life we live.   _____

14. Christ became "sin for us" when God placed our sins on Christ's account.   _____

15. The statement, "Christ is our righteousness," is true because God has placed Christ's righteousness to our account. _____

☐ **I have memorized Romans 1:16.**

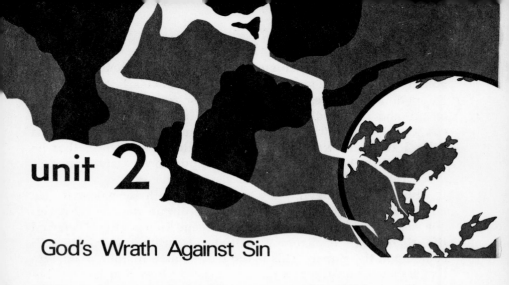

unit 2

God's Wrath Against Sin

Romans 1:18 presents a truth that should strike fear to the hearts of men. The words are: "For the wrath of God is revealed from heaven against all ungodliness and unrighteousness of men, who hold the truth in unrighteousness." Men have sought to avoid this truth by telling us that God is a God of love but not a God of wrath.

If God had no wrath against sin, then He would love everything including all that men do—their filthy talking, their hatred of each other and their murders. God could not be God if He loved evil, or even condoned it. It is true that love is an attribute of God. It is part of His character; God as to His nature is love. It is the very expression of His being. But God is righteous; consequently, where sin is there must be wrath against sin. The attributes of God are properly balanced in His Person. He is not unbalanced like men, who are as they are because of sin.

It is not dealing fairly with the Scriptures to take verses that speak of God's love and leave out those that deal with His wrath.

There must be no misunderstanding of what God's wrath is. It should never be confused with man's wrath, which is a sinful thing.

God's wrath is not a sudden fit of temper, neither is it a desire for revenge. These things are sin, and we cannot attribute sin to God. God's wrath is a fixed attitude of opposition toward all unrighteousness. This attitude never changes. It will culminate in righteous judgment upon all who finally and completely reject God's offer of love.

17

God will not shelter sin and He will not excuse it. God abhors sin, but He loves the sinner. That is clearly seen in that He made a way of escape for the sinner from the consequences of sin, and provided such a wonderful salvation in Christ. We can see God's attitude toward the sinner in such a passage as John 3:16 where we read that "God so loved the world that he gave his only begotten Son." His attitude toward sin, however, is entirely different.

Sin is of the Devil, and God in His wrath is against it. He will never tolerate it regardless of the circumstances. If a sinner continues in sin, refusing to accept God's gift of eternal life, then God's unchanging attitude of wrath toward sin will come upon the sinner. This is the truth stated in John 3:36: "He that believeth on the Son hath everlasting life: and he that believeth not the Son shall not see life; but the wrath of God [the unchangeable attitude of God against sin] abideth on him." In other words, when the sinner clings to his sin and refuses God's offer of mercy, then sin and the sinner are one so far as the wrath of God is concerned. When a person persists in identifying himself with sin in this way, he comes under the unchanging attitude of God against sin.

God's Wrath Is Known to Men

God has made known His attitude against sin, for that is the meaning of the expression "the wrath of God is revealed from heaven" (1:18). This is further borne out by Romans 1:32 where we are told, "Who knowing the judgment of God, that they which commit such things are worthy of death, not only do the same, but have pleasure in them that do them."

God has revealed His attitude against sin in that He sent His only begotten Son to die on the cross for us. Calvary demonstrates God's unchanging abhorrence of sin as nothing else does.

God's wrath is against all ungodliness. Ungodliness simply means "living without God." We read these words in Romans 1:21-23: "Because that, when they knew God, they glorified him not as God, neither were thankful; but became vain in their imaginations, and their foolish heart was darkened. Professing themselves to be wise, they became fools, And changed the glory of the uncorruptible God into an image made like to corruptible man, and to birds, and fourfooted beasts, and creeping things." Men have always had a certain amount of truth concerning God,

18

and yet the majority of them have not glorified Him as God, neither have they been thankful, but have sought to live without Him. This is the history of man from the Fall to the present moment.

When men live ungodly lives, they show that they are living without God. When they live unrighteous lives, they produce not righteous acts, but evil deeds. Without God it is impossible for men to produce righteousness. By nature we are sold under sin, and only God can effect our release.

God's wrath is revealed against those who hold down the truth in unrighteousness. Those of whom this passage speaks are not ignorant of God's existence, but in spite of what they know they press on in their evil living.

Four Facts Concerning Wrath

We may summarize the truth of Romans 1:18 under four thoughts.

1. God's wrath is contemporary; that is, God's wrath is on men now. It is revealed now; it has been revealed in history; and the record of His judgment against sin is to be found all through the Scriptures. The climax of the revelation of God's wrath against sin is seen in the cross, where Christ died for our sins. Furthermore, the prophecies of the Bible indicate that certain judgments are yet to come. In fact, the worst judgments on the world of mankind are still future. However, God's wrath is revealed not only in the past and in the future, but it is also expressed here and now.

2. God's wrath is all inclusive. It is against all evil. Men try to put sin into different categories, saying one is a big sin and another is a little sin, but to God all sin is moral evil. God is even against the thought of sin.

3. The wrath of God is absolutely inescapable. It is sometimes possible for men who have committed crimes to escape the wrath of human courts through clever manipulation by lawyers who know how to take advantage of technicalities in the law, but no unsaved person can ever escape the wrath of God. He knows us through and through. "Neither is there any creature that is not manifest in his sight: but all things are naked and opened unto the eyes of him with whom we have to do" (Heb. 4:13). Vengeance belongs unto God. It is a fearful

thing to fall into His hands, unrepentant and rebellious against His government.

God's wrath is justifiable. It is not an arbitrarily-planned vengeance. It is based on man's deliberate sin of irreverence for God, his unjust acts toward his fellow men, and his refusal of God's love.

What Men Know About God

The apostle now takes up the subject of knowledge that is common to all men concerning God. The words are: "Because that which may be known of God is manifest in them; for God hath shewed it unto them. For the invisible things of him from the creation of the world are clearly seen, being understood by the things that are made, even his eternal power and Godhead; so that they are without excuse" (1:19,20).

God is speaking here of those who have refused His gift of salvation. They are guilty not only of sin, but of holding down the truth in unrighteousness. Just in what sense these persons know God is clearly stated here. They have an inner revelation of God, for the Word says this knowledge of God is "manifest in them." There is an innate, inborn knowledge of God in every man. It is engraved on the constitution of his very nature. This fact is evident in the religious tendencies seen in all peoples. We may say that some persons are irreligious, but in reality they are not. Man is a religious creature.

We often say that the Communist is irreligious, but such is not the case. He is anti-God. He is against the God of the Bible, but that is simply because He wants to exalt something else in the place of God. This religious quality is inherent in man, and the Communist can no more escape it than any other person. A man may claim to be an atheist, and say, "There is no God"; but deep down in the heart of every man is the consciousness that God exists.

Not only does man know in his own heart that there is a God, but there is an external revelation of the existence of God in creation. The invisible things of God, that is, the things which the natural eye cannot see, are nevertheless understood to exist "by the things that are made." That which may be known of God in creation is stated in the next words: "Even his eternal power and Godhead." When a man is honest with himself he cannot but admit that God is the Creator with unlimited power.

A noted evolutionist once said, "Give me power and give me matter, and I will show you all things." He was not willing to acknowledge that God has the power, or better yet, IS the Power and Creator of all matter.

We cannot help but see God's handiwork as we look around us. When studying this passage, I took time to look around my room and saw the plant life in it. I glanced outside and saw the birds. I could not help but think how everything around me points to the mighty power of God as Creator, and shows His wisdom in providing all things needed for the present and the future.

We have what we sometimes call the "law of cause and effect." This means that for every effect there must be an adequate cause. Such an outstanding effect as the universe itself demands for its cause a Being who has eternal power and divine attributes.

Whatever a man sows, he will reap. Man cannot ignore God or sneer at Him and not be called to account for his conduct.

What Nature Reveals

The revelation God has given of Himself in nature is adequate to show that He exists, and that He is the Creator, Designer and Provider for His universe. Romans 1:20 tells us that these things "are clearly seen."

We hear people speak of some kind of Almighty power, though they may not define God as a Person. The intimate personal revelation of God comes through the Word, and through Jesus Christ. Revelation is the source of these truths, not creation. Yet men can know that God is, and that He is good. Even the heathen know this. Missionaries have told how they have approached heathen men and women and asked, "Why do you worship the Devil? Why do you not worship God?" The answer is generally the same no matter where it is asked. "Why worship God? He is good. He is not going to do us any harm." So, instead of worshiping God, they worship evil things, whom they fear will harm them and their families. Such people do not see a plan of redemption, but they are conscious of their sin and of their need of salvation. When men are honest with themselves in the light of their own consciences, they will have to admit that they are lost. Therefore, God is just in His condemnation of men.

The words "without excuse" mean that man is without defense for his action. Man will never be able to defend himself when he stands in the presence of God. The evidence is all against man.

The personal revelation of God in redemption is seen only in Christ and is revealed through the Bible. The revelation of God in nature and to the heart of man is limited, but adequate to the extent of revealing that God is a God of power and of might, and that men should worship Him.

Memory Assignment:
Memorize Romans 1:18.

EXAMINATION

In the right-hand margin write "True" or "False" after each of the following statements:

1. If God had no wrath against sin He would love even men's sinful acts. _____

2. The Bible's descriptions of God's wrath prove that His righteousness is more prominent than His love. _____

3. God's wrath is greater for big sins than for insignificant sins. _____

4. A righteous judgment of unbelievers will be the final demonstration of God's wrath. _____

5. Because God adhors sin He must logically hate those who sin. _____

In the blank space at the right-hand margin write the letter of the correct or most nearly correct answer.

6. God's attitude toward the sinner is shown specifically in:
   (a) Romans 1:18
   (b) John 3:16
   (c) John 3:36 _____

7. If a sinner continues in sin, refusing God's gift of eternal life, God says:
   (a) he shall not perish, but have everlasting life
   (b) he will have another chance after death
   (c) he shall not see life, but God's wrath is upon him

   _____

8. Jesus' death on Calvary reveals:
   (a) God's readiness to excuse man's sin
   (b) God's love for the sinner and abhorrence of sin
   (c) God's forgiveness of the sins of all men, whether or not they accept it _____

9. Ungodliness simply means:
   (a) living without God
   (b) refusing to believe in God
   (c) uncertainty as to God's existence _____

10. God's wrath:
    (a) is on men now
    (b) is reserved only for the final judgment
    (c) is against only the worst categories of sin _____

Complete the following:

11. Although a criminal may sometimes escape punishment by taking advantage of legal technicalities, the wrath of God is _____.

12. Romans 1:19 tells us that every man has an inner _____ of God.

13. The scientific law of _____ and _____ indicates very plainly that creation must have had a Creator.

14. In view of the revelation of God described in Romans 1:19,20, men are _____ _____ for rejecting God and living ungodly lives.

15. The personal revelation of God in redemption is seen only in _____ and is revealed through the _____.

☐ **I have memorized Romans 1:18.**

24

unit 3

Man Without God

"Because that, when they knew God, they glorified him not as God, neither were thankful: but became vain in their imaginations, and their foolish heart was darkened. Professing themselves to be wise, they became fools, And changed the glory of the uncorruptible God into an image made like to corruptible man, and to birds, and fourfooted beasts, and creeping things" (Rom. 1:21-23).

Sin's Progression

These verses tell us of the downward steps man took as he plunged himself into spiritual and moral ruin.

The first step was that of impiety. Men "glorified him not as God." They refused to honor and reverence God.

The second downward step was that of ingratitude: "Neither were they thankful." They knew they were fully dependent upon God, but they did not praise Him for it. We are dependent upon God for the very air we breathe from moment to moment. All around us are the evidences of His provisions, fully adequate for all men. He keeps, provides and protects, and yet the record is that man was not thankful. In his ingratitude he abused the very gifts God gave him.

The third downward step was that man became vain in his imaginations or reasoning. This was not only true of man immediately after the Fall, but it is also true of men today. Reason is substituted for revelation. Instead of trusting God, man seeks to reason his way through this world. This attitude is even found in Christian circles, and wherever it is found, it always leads away from God. Man thinks he knows more than God, but his reasoning ends in futility. It ends in nothingness for man, and causes him to be unsuccessful and devoid of satisfaction.

The next downward step is described in the words: "Their foolish heart was darkened." Men, boasting in their reasoning, actually became unintelligent and without proper understanding. The heart, which is the seat of the feelings, is also considered the place of moral choice. Man's moral choices were of the wrong kind. That is why mankind has gone further and further into sin. As the Scripture says, "Professing themselves to be wise, they became fools." "Professing" here means "pretending" —claiming something that is not real.

Wisdom comes from God alone and when men turned away from God they became fools. The word "fool" means "foolish, stupid or dull." And that is what God says concerning man who refuses to acknowledge Him even though evidences of God are plainly revealed in nature.

In spite of all this, man could not get away from what he was by nature with regard to his religious desires. He still wanted to worship something, but he perverted that desire, for in turning away from God and becoming a fool he "changed the glory of the uncorruptible God into an image made like to corruptible man, and to birds, and fourfooted beasts, and creeping things." Man manufactured his own gods. The incorruptible God was made into a corruptible god—and that on a descending scale. First, man with images of man, then birds, then beasts, and finally snakes. Such is the descent of man as the result of sin. This is the record of how man degraded himself.

The Consequences of Sin

The law or principle of spiritual harvest is seen in the next section of the first chapter of Romans. This law is stated for us in Galatians 6:7 where we read: "Whatsoever a man soweth, that shall he also reap." If a man sows to the flesh, he will reap corruption. If he sows to the Spirit, he will reap life everlasting. The record in the latter part of Romans 1 is of men who sowed to their fallen natures and the awful consequences that followed.

This passage of Scripture does not make pleasant reading, but it describes what has happened to man down through the years.

My father was a missionary among the Hopi Indians in Arizona and in the course of his work he translated some of the Bible to them. One day as he was reading the first part of the Book of Romans to some 50 or 60 Indians, an old chief got up and called him a liar. He declared that such statements were not in the Bible. My father assured him that they were and that the portion he had read was the first chapter of Romans. Still the old chief insisted that such could not have been in the Bible. He felt that the missionary had been told the story of their lives by a converted chief and had read it to them as though it were a part of the Bible.

That was a startling confession of conditions among the Indians. They admitted that this section of Romans was a complete description of the way the pagan Indians lived.

The picture becomes more alarming when we realize that these conditions are the result of God having abandoned men to their own sinful ways. He will not force men to worship Him. They either do it willingly or not at all. God will not violate a man's will in this matter. But when men choose to forsake God and worship the creature rather than the Creator, then God gives them over to the control of the sinful things they prefer.

This does not mean that God merely stood aside and let men continue to go the wrong way. It was not that God permitted all this to take place; He actually passed a judicial judgment upon them. God delivered them up to these things as an act of judgment and punishment.

Such is a foretaste of hell itself. Sin begets more sin and is followed by greater darkness. Man's heart is hardened, and he hurries on to more fearful degrees of depravity.

Judicial Judgments

Three times in this closing portion of Romans 1 we read the expression, "Wherefore God also gave them up." The first of these appears in verse 24: "Wherefore God also gave them up to uncleanness through the lusts of their own hearts, to dishonour their own bodies between themselves: Who changed the truth of God into a lie, and worshipped and served the creature more than the Creator, who is blessed for ever." God gave them up to sexual lusts and perversions. They became brutish: their chief concern was to satisfy their own passions.

They perverted God-given powers to satisfy the cravings of their fallen natures. This was the direct result of having changed the truth of God into a lie, and having exalted the creature to the place rightfully belonging to the Creator.

The second occurrence of this phrase, "God gave them up," is found in verse 26. "For this cause God gave them up into vile affections: for even their women did change the natural use unto that which is against nature: And likewise also the men, leaving the natural use of the woman, burned in their lust one toward another: men with men working that which is unseemly, and receiving in themselves that recompence of their error which was meet." When men gave God up, it was in order that they might indulge their own passions. So God gave them over to these things which became vile and unnatural affections. "Homosexuality" is the one word that describes this condition accurately. Practicing acts which were contrary to nature, these received the results which were bound to follow such conduct. They paid for their own sins in the sense of reaping what they sowed. And men who persist in such things will continue to reap this terrible harvest, not only in time but in eternity, for the Word says, "The wages of sin is death."

The third occurrence of this expression is found in verse 28. "And even as they did not like to retain God in their knowledge, God gave them over to a reprobate mind, to do those things which are not convenient." God abandoned them to a reprobate mind, one which is unfit to distinguish between right and wrong. It is a mind that is warped with regard to moral judgment. The very opposite of this takes place when men are born again, for then they are given "a new mind." God renews the mind of those who trust Christ so that they can think properly. On the other hand, those who persist in sin and refuse to retain God in their knowledge are given over to a degenerated mind.

When God gives a man over to a reprobate mind, that man's mind is like an abandoned building such as a barn or a shed. It soon becomes the home of rats and snakes which live as they desire, with no one to curb them. That is what happens to the mind that God abandons. It is open to every kind of evil thing, of which a list is given in the closing verses of this chapter. The mind becomes permeated with every kind of evil purpose and desire imaginable.

Such minds are "filled with all unrighteousness, fornication, wickedness, covetousness, maliciousness; full of envy, murder, debate, deceit, malignity; whisperers, Backbiters, haters of God, despiteful, proud, boasters, inventors of evil things, disobedient to parents, Without understanding, covenant breakers, without natural affection, implacable, unmerciful." What a terrible description this is! It does not mean that every individual who has turned from God has all of these tendencies prominent in his life, but he exhibits one or more of them.

Unrighteousness

The apostle speaks of every kind of unrighteousness being expressed. This is seen in the violation of justice among men and in the constant tendency to inflict evil upon others.

He also mentions covetousness which is expressed in greed and the desire to have things regardless of the cost to the other fellow.

Maliciousness refers to wilful and deliberate harm done to one's neighbor.

Envy is a sister to jealousy—a robber of all spiritual blessings. Even Christian people have missed spiritual blessings because of envy.

Murder also appears in this list. We are not overstating it when we say that if the sins mentioned previous to murder are given free rein, they may lead to murder.

There are words here that describe a spirit of dissatisfaction. Such things as quarreling and fighting and sedition are resistance to lawful authority. The sad part of this is that these are not confined to the world. They can be seen at times in the church. But wherever they are found, they work like cancer.

Whisperers are also mentioned. There are gossipers, people who delight in stirring up trouble. A backbiter is one who slanders another, not openly but secretly. All the haters of God may not express their hatred in words, but they eventually show it in the lives they live. Though they may even tend to be religious, deep in their hearts they do not want God.

Such also become despiteful and overbearing, brutal, haughty, swollen with pride, arrogant, boastful, vain braggarts.

They are also inventors of evil things, introducing new crimes against their fellowmen.

The disobedience to parents spoken of in this passage goes beyond the aspect of rebellion. It shows the inborn hatred to lawful authority. Disobedience to parents is a result of the revolt against God. This produces anarchy in society and shows itself to be against any kind of authority, whether civil or religious.

Such people are also without understanding, void of spiritual insight into spiritual or moral things. They cannot be trusted; they are covenant breakers, faithless, liars, unreliable, with no sense of honor in dealing with others. The utter selfishness and cruelty of their character is seen in that they are without natural affection, implacable, unmerciful. They have no love even for their own flesh and blood. Much of this is being seen today in individuals and in nations. No mercy is shown; men are utterly heartless toward each other, pitiless in their suppression of whatever displeases them.

The final verse of this chapter shows that such persons are confirmed in their own unholiness. God describes them as "knowing the judgment of God, that they which commit such things are worthy of death, not only do the same, but have pleasure in them that do them." Although knowing the judgments of God, such persons recklessly cast caution to the winds and go all out for sin. They boast in their evil and encourage others to do likewise, applauding them when they do. Such blind rebellion seems hard to believe, but this is God's description not only of past generations, but of the generation in which we now live.

But as black as this picture is, God has a remedy for each person who will turn to Him seeking forgiveness through Christ. No wonder Paul was not ashamed of the gospel of Christ. It takes sinners such as are described in this portion and makes them fit to stand before God.

Memory Assignment:
Memorize Romans 1:21.

EXAMINATION

Complete the following:

1. The first step downward toward man's spiritual and moral ruin was _____.

2. The second downward step is described by the words, "neither were they _____."

3. The third downward step was man's substituting _____ for revelation.

4. Professing to be wise, men in their downward spiral actually became _____.

5. To satisfy his need for worship, degraded man "changed the glory of the incorruptible God into an _____ made like to corruptible _____."

In the right-hand margin write "True" or "False" after each of the following statements:

6. The principle of spiritual harvest is stated in the words: "Seek ye first the kingdom of God, and all these things shall be added unto you." _____

7. Man's sinfulness described at the end of Romans 1 resulted because God merely stood aside and let men continue to go the wrong way. _____

8. When men exalted the creature to the place rightfully belonging to the Creator they became interested only in satisfying their own passions. _____

9. The punishment involved in God's giving men up to their sins was that they would reap the results of their sinful conduct. _____

10. Those who persist in sin and refuse to retain God in their knowledge become the objects of God's special care. _____

In the blank space at the right-hand margin write the letter of the correct or most nearly correct answer.

11. The mind which God abandons:
    (a) becomes able to exercise true freedom of choice
    (b) becomes able to understand the natural and scientific facts of life
    (c) becomes permeated with every evil purpose and desire imaginable _____

12. The sins listed in Romans 1:29-31:
    (a) are sins which a true Christian cannot commit
    (b) are all to be found in the life of every unbeliever
    (c) are sins which result from a mind abandoned by God
    _____

13. Sins which, regrettably, are often committed by Christians are:
    (a) envy and pride
    (b) fornication and murder
    (c) hatred of God and disobedience to parents   _____

14. God describes those who are confirmed in their own unholiness as:
    (a) ignorant of the consequences of sin
    (b) eager to encourage others to do evil
    (c) secretly fearful of the outcome of sin   _____

15. Persons such as described in Romans 1:29-31 can find God's remedy for their sin:
    (a) by changing their habits and seeking to live up to God's standard
    (b) by attending church and becoming involved in its activities
    (c) by confessing their sins to Jesus Christ, asking for His complete forgiveness, and trusting Him for new spiritual life and right standing before God.   _____

☐ **I have memorized Romans 1:21.**

unit 4

God's Principles of Judgment

"Therefore thou art inexcusable, O man, whosoever thou art that judgest: for wherein thou judgest another, thou condemnest thyself; for thou that judgest doest the same things. But we are sure that the judgment of God is according to truth against them which commit such things. And thinkest thou this, O man, that judgest them which do such things, and doest the same, that thou shalt escape the judgment of God?" (Rom. 2:1-3).

The Moralist

The moralist of Romans 2 is one who judges another on the basis of his own moral standards. He does not know God's righteousness and condemnation of all men as sinners. He sees sin as only a matter of degree, and justifies himself on the basis that his conduct is not as bad as that of some others. God's standard of righteousness, however, is not based on what men think but on who God is. He is holy and His standards must be equal to His character. He could not raise a standard of righteousness that is less than His own righteousness.

Man-made Standards

The moral man of Romans 2 is sometimes found where we would least expect him. He is commonly found among church members, and he can be found even in churches where the gospel is believed and preached. There are those who belong to Bible-believing churches who look down on the so-called liberals or modernists because they have rejected the foundational truths of the Christian faith, including the Word of God itself. Yet such a member of the Bible-believing church could be one who gives mere lip service to these things and is depending upon his church connections and his moral life for salvation.

The same spirit can be seen in the person who despises those who do not belong to his particular denomination. He may believe that his group has all the truth, and that the others do not have any. Or again, it may be that the one who belongs to a church looks down on someone who does not go to church at all. But the standard used by all of these is a standard of their own devising.

There are many people who base their morality on what they are socially, where they go to church, and the kind of standards they seek to uphold. The important thing, however, is not what our self-estimates are, but what God says concerning these matters.

The Same Condemnation

God's answer to the moralist is that he faces the same condemnation as the one he despises. The inconsistencies in the conduct of the moralist show him to be basically the same in character as the out and out sinner of Romans 1.

We are all sinners by birth. All have sinned.

So then, it is not the question of how good we are in our own eyes. We are all in the same class so far as God is concerned, because we have not met His standards. In fact, we cannot meet those standards in ourselves; they can be met only through the power of God. God offers us His righteousness as a gift through faith in the Lord Jesus Christ. But that righteousness will never become ours until we first recognize our own lack of righteousness.

Because God does not bring swift judgment on the moralists who reject His offer of mercy is no reason for them to think that He is pleased with them. Romans 2:4 says, "Or despisest thou the riches of his goodness and forbearance and longsuffering; not knowing that the goodness of God leadeth thee to repentance?"

Delay of judgment in a case like this is not an endorsement of the person, but a sign of the kindness and longsuffering of God, the purpose of which is to bring the sinner to repentance.

The warning of God continues in verse 5: "But after thy hardness and impenitent heart treasurest up unto thyself wrath against the day of wrath and revelation of the righteous judgment of God." Men must not ignore or trifle with God's pleading and grace. If they do, they are heaping up extra judgment for the day of judgment.

The Righteousness of God's Judgment

God's judgments are righteous. Romans 2:5 speaks of the "revelation of the righteous judgment of God." This is summed up for us in four phrases taken from four different verses in this chapter. The first of these is in verse 6: "Who will render to every man according to his deeds." In verse 11 are these words: "For there is no respect of persons with God." Then in verse 12 we are told, "As many as have sinned without law shall also perish without law." Finally, in verse 16 Paul declares: "In the day when God shall judge the secrets of men by Jesus Christ according to my gospel."

God will judge men righteously, basing His conclusions on their deeds. He will show no partiality; no favoritism whatsoever. Judgment will be based on the light they have received and how they have followed it, and on the gospel of Jesus Christ.

Judgment According to Deeds

The Scriptures are clear about man not being saved by his conduct; but the things he does are a good index of whether or not the Spirit of God has been able to do a saving work within his heart. What a man really is can generally be known by what he does.

As a further explanation of the judgment according to deeds, verse 7 says, "To them who by patient continuance in well doing seek for glory and honour and immortality, eternal life." The persons seeking the glory and honor of Christ are the ones who recognize God's gift of salvation. They have sought immortality [incorruption] and God gives them eternal life, not for what they do, but because they have placed their faith in Christ. This is unmistakably clear from what is said in Romans 3:22: "Even the righteousness of God which is by faith of Jesus Christ unto all and upon all them that believe: for there is no difference."

The impossibility of a man earning salvation by his deeds is stated emphatically in a passage beginning with Romans 5:6: "For when we were yet without strength, in due time Christ died for the ungodly." In verse 8 the apostle says, "But God commendeth his love toward us, in that, while we were yet sinners, Christ died for us." The next two verses drive home the points already made: "Much more then, being now justified by his blood, we shall be saved from wrath through him. For if, when we were enemies, we were reconciled to God by the death of his Son, much more, being reconciled, we shall be saved by his life."

God Is No Respecter of Persons

God plays no favorites. He does not consider one person to be holier than another because of a difference in their outward behavior. Whereas man judges largely by what he sees in the conduct of others, God looks upon the heart. A number of Scripture illustrations bear this out.

In the third chapter of John's Gospel we read of Nicodemus who had a high position in the religious circles of Israel. Our Lord made it very clear to him that he must be born again. "Except a man be born again, he cannot see the kingdom of God," were the words which startled this Jewish leader.

The Saviour said very plainly to the scribes and Pharisees of His day: "And ye will not come to me, that ye might have life" (John 5:40). He was simply saying to these men that they were shut out from salvation because they refused to come to Him. Later, as recorded in John 6:37, our Saviour stated: "And him that cometh to me I will in no wise cast out." All men have the same need of salvation, and God offers all men the same way of salvation in Christ. He is no respecter of persons.

God Judges According to Light

God judges men according to the knowledge He has given them. In the first chapter of Romans, we saw how quickly the first great civilization of men became increasingly evil. They never heard many of the Biblical truths that we hear today. Nevertheless, they knew inwardly through the conscience and outwardly in the things they saw around them in creation that God is the Creator and Provider of life. They had light, and they will be judged according to the way they used it. God's judgment is a righteous judgment, because He deals with men according to their response to what light He has given them.

There is a difference in the amount of light different people have, and yet all have sufficient light so that they know God exists and that they themselves are lost.

Those whom we consider the most backward peoples illustrate this for us. Whether we go to Africa or to the Indians of South America, we find them bringing offerings to their gods. Why? Because, according to the light of their conscience, they know they are lost. They go against this light, however, by not coming to the true God. Instead, they try to sooth their consciences by playing into the hands of the Evil One.

I am sure, on the basis of the Word (John 7:17), that if they wanted more light God would see that someone would bring it to them; if they live up to the light they have, He will see that they have additional truth. That phase of this matter we leave in His hands. This is no reason, however, for us to be complacent about their salvation and place all the responsibility for their lost condition on them.

I believe that we as Christians have the blood of many of the lost on our hands. We have light concerning them. We know they are in darkness and that God has commanded us to give them the Light of Life. It is our responsibility. We who know Christ are debtors to those who know Him not. God lays upon our shoulders the obligation of reaching the lost with the gospel.

Judgment According to the Gospel

God will also judge men according to the gospel. The gospel to which Paul referred is clearly set forth in the first four verses of I Corinthians 15. "Moreover, brethren, I declare unto you the gospel which I preached unto you, which also ye have received, and wherein ye stand: By which also ye are saved, if ye keep in memory what I preached unto you, unless ye have believed in vain. For I delivered unto you first of all that which I also received, how that Christ died for our sins according to the scriptures: And that he was buried, and that he rose again the third day according to the scriptures."

This is the gospel. Christ died, He was buried, He rose again, and the salvation He provided is ours for believing in Him or receiving what He offers us. All men are to be judged on the basis of that gospel.

God is dealing with religious people in the second chapter of Romans and He lays stress on the fact that even though the religious man prides himself on what he does, he is a lost man without Christ. There is no spiritual difference among men apart from the difference Christ makes. The difference He makes is stated in Romans 3:26: "To declare, I say, at this time his righteousness: that he might be just, and the justifier of him which believeth in Jesus."

Apart from Christ, man cannot be righteous before God. How a person may come to Christ is explained in Romans 10:9,10: "That if thou shalt confess with thy mouth the Lord Jesus, and shalt believe in thine heart that God hath raised him from the dead, thou shalt be saved. For with the heart man believeth unto righteousness: and with the mouth confession is made unto salvation."

Greater Condemnation

In accordance with what we have already seen concerning the judgments of God, we know that those who have the Word of God and reject it will have the greater condemnation. This is illustrated for us in a number of Scriptures. There were cities in Galilee which heard our Saviour speak, and also heard His disciples. These cities had the truth of the Word of God, but the Lord Jesus found it necessary to denounce them for the rejection of the signs done among them and the truth proclaimed to them.

The record is: "Then began he to upbraid the cities wherein most of his mighty works were done, because they repented not: Woe unto thee, Chorazin! woe unto thee, Bethsaida! for if the mighty works, which were done in you, had been done in Tyre and Sidon, they would have repented long ago in sackcloth and ashes. But I say unto you, It shall be more tolerable for Tyre and Sidon at the day of judgment, than for you. And thou, Capernaum, which art exalted unto heaven, shalt be brought down to hell: for if the mighty works, which have been done in thee, had been done in Sodom, it would have remained until this day. But I say unto you, That it shall be more tolerable for the land of Sodom in the day of judgment, than for thee" (Matt. 11:20-24).

Another passage dealing with this same truth is Matthew 12:41,42: "The men of Nineveh shall rise in judgment with this generation, and shall condemn it: because they repented at the preaching of Jonas; and, behold, a greater than Jonas is here. The queen of the south shall rise up in the judgment with this generation, and shall condemn it: for she came from the uttermost parts of the earth to hear the wisdom of Solomon; and, behold, a greater than Solomon is here." Simply stated, when men turn from the light of the gospel, the more severe will be the judgment against them. God is absolutely righteous in His judgments.

Memory Assignment:
Memorize Romans 2:4.

EXAMINATION

In the right-hand margin write "True" or "False" after each of the following statements:

1. The moralist described in Romans 2 is one who judges others according to God's standard of right and wrong.

2. God's standard of right and wrong is based on the conduct of the majority of people.

3. The attitude of the moral man of Romans 2 would never be found in a Bible-believing church.

4. Social standing, church membership and high moral standards are the important things in determining one's righteousness before God.

5. God's answer to the moralist is that he faces the same condemnation as those he despises.

Complete the following:

6. Any delay in God's judgment is only a sign of God's _____, as He seeks to bring the sinner to repentance.

7. In God's judgment He "will render to every man according to his _____."

8. With God there is no _____ of persons.

9. Judgment will be based on the _____ a person has received, and on the _____.

10. A person is not saved by his _____, which is actually a sign of whether he is saved or not.

In the blank space at the right-hand margin write the letter of the correct or most nearly correct answer.

11. God offers salvation to all men:
    (a) on the condition of their conduct
    (b) on the condition of the light they have received
    (c) on the condition of their response to Jesus Christ
    _____

12. The Word of God indicates (John 7:17) that if a person will live up to the light he has, even though he has not heard the gospel:
    (a) God will save him according to his works
    (b) God will see that someone will take the gospel to him
    (c) God will give him a chance to turn to Christ after death
    _____

13. The only real spiritual difference between men is:
    (a) the possession or lack of the righteousness received from Christ through faith in Him
    (b) obedience or disobedience to the laws of God
    (c) belief in God as opposed to atheism
    _____

14. According to Romans 10:9,10 one of the conditions for being saved is to believe in the heart:
    (a) that Jesus died
    (b) that God raised Jesus from the dead
    (c) that Jesus will come again
    _____

15. According to the words of Jesus, when men reject the light of the gospel:
    (a) they are freed from any further obligation to God
    (b) God has promised to be merciful in judging them
    (c) their judgment will be more severe than if they had never heard the gospel
    _____

☐   **I have memorized Romans 2:4.**

unit 5

The Jew and His Advantages

In Romans 2:17 the subject of the Jew is brought before us. "Behold, thou art called a Jew, and restest in the law, and makest thy boast of God." This section of Scripture presents the various matters in which the Jew felt he was superior to the Gentile. There is no question but what the Jewish people had advantages in having the Word of God and in having seen God's great power demonstrated time and again on their behalf. Yet, this very light brought greater condemnation to those of that nation who turned away from faith in Christ.

The message here most certainly reaches beyond the Jew and speaks to the Christians of our day. This same truth is applicable to those of us who have enjoyed the Word of God and rich blessings from His hand. The very thing in which we boast can be the ground for our condemnation as it was in the day when our Saviour ministered on the earth. In speaking to the scribes and Pharisees of His day, He said, "Do not think that I will accuse you to the Father: there is one that accuseth you, even Moses, in whom ye trust" (John 5:45).

Like the Jew of old we boast as though God were our private property, that God is on our side, and that we are always in the right. We are inclined to boast that we are God-fearing people. But let us beware, for the very thing we boast in can make our condemnation the greater. While we proclaim freedom, we leave Christ out of our lives; but there can be no real freedom without Him. We present Him as an example and as a great teacher, but not as the Saviour. We have undoubtedly been greatly favored of God in material things and also in freedom to hear and to spread the gospel message; but this also carries with it a great responsibility.

Paul says that the Jew of old claimed to know God and approved the things which are more excellent, "being instructed out of the law" (v. 18). We as a people are sure that the will of God is that the nations of the world should all be free. We would like to see the yoke of Communism broken and enslaved peoples liberated. This is a worthy goal, but as a nation we leave out the most important freedom of all—freedom from sin's guilt and power which only Christ can give us.

Paul's further description accurately fits Christendom today: "And art confident that thou thyself art a guide of the blind, a light of them which are in darkness, An instructor of the foolish, a teacher of babes, which hast the form of knowledge and of the truth in the law. Thou therefore which teachest another, teachest thou not thyself? thou that preachest a man should not steal, dost thou steal?" (vv. 19-21).

Many will protest that they do not steal, and they will be right if they are thinking of stealing from a store or from a bank. But there are even Christians who steal God's time and His money and impose on God's longsuffering. God has given to Christians the responsibility of spreading the gospel around the world, but altogether too many store it up for themselves, live in their own selfish ways, and heap up treasures for this life instead of for God.

A grave indictment of such conduct is given in verse 24: "For the name of God is blasphemed among the Gentiles through you, as it is written." Remember that Nathan charged David when he committed his great sin with these words: "By this deed thou hast given great occasion to the enemies of the Lord to blaspheme" (II Sam. 12:14).

Voltaire, that well-known French infidel, declared that he revolted against Christianity because of the kind of things he saw in those who claimed to be Christians.

When people have what is only mere religion, it does them no good and can do others a great amount of harm. The Jews had a religion, the only religion God ever gave to men. The Jews were proud of their religious ceremonies and boasted particularly in the sign of circumcision. Of that, however, the apostle says, "For circumcision verily profiteth, if thou keep the law: but if thou be a breaker of the law, thy circumcision is made uncircumcision" (Rom. 2:25). The only profit in circumcision lay in keeping the whole law. To break one part was to break all of it. In that case, circumcision was made uncircumcision. In other words, it was of no use or value whatsoever.

God Looks at the Heart

The next step in the argument is, "Therefore if the uncircumcision [Gentiles—those who have not been circumcised] keep the righteousness of the law, shall not his uncircumcision [his lack of ceremonial practices] be counted for circumcision?" (2:26). What is necessary is something far more than mere external ceremonies. It is our heart condition that God is speaking of here, something that goes far deeper than outward religious conduct.

So many people divide their lives up into different departments. They have a place for recreation, a place for work, a time for sleep—and a certain place is reserved for religion. What God is looking for is something entirely different. A tacked-on religious life does not meet His requirements. He wants a heart attitude toward Him that will govern all phases of our lives— something that will meet His approval for all time and eternity.

This is clearly set forth in the New Testament Book of Colossians. In verses 6 and 7 in the second chapter we read: "As ye have therefore received Christ Jesus the Lord, so walk ye in him: Rooted and built up in him, and established in the faith, as ye have been taught, abounding therein with thanksgiving." Then in verses 9-11 it is said of Christ: "For in Him dwelleth all the fulness of the Godhead bodily. And ye are complete in him, which is the head of all principality and power: In whom also ye are circumcised with the circumcision made without hands, in putting off the body of the sins of the flesh by the circumcision of Christ."

These verses reveal that when we receive Jesus Christ as Saviour, He has already accomplished for us what outward circumcision was merely a sign of. He has purified, cleansed and forgiven us of our sins. In addition—and this is very essential to grasp—He gives us a new, holy life, He himself being that life.

Someone may protest and say, "I do not understand that."

There is much about Christian truth that none of us understands. In fact, there is a great deal about life in general that no one understands. But do we disbelieve certain things merely because we do not understand them? God asks us to accept by faith these things provided in Christ for us. It is not a matter of understanding but of believing.

God proved to the Jews that they had utterly failed in what they were seeking to do outwardly. On the other hand, God assured them (and us) that when Christ comes into the heart He does His work first inwardly, and then shows the evidence of it outwardly. He separates us from sin. Its guilt is removed, its judgment can never come upon us, and its bondage is broken. He lives in us the holy and godly life that God requires. This is only possible to any of us, however, if we receive Christ.

Perhaps as you read this you are asking, "How can I have Christ?" The Bible says that we are to receive Him. Perhaps you ask another question, "How can I receive Him if He is a person sitting at the right hand of God the Father?" The problem is that we in our limited experience think of a person as having bodily form, and weighing so many pounds. It is true that the Scriptures say Christ is in a glorified body at the right hand of God. But it is also true that Christ is present everywhere, and He can live in us as well as in His present glorified body in the heavens.

In Him dwells the fullness of the Godhead bodily. He is the head of everything. He is the life of the believer. You cannot see the life that is in me, yet it is there. One of these days the report may be given that I am dead. I would not say it that way for I am going to continue living. The only difference will be that I will have moved out of this body and the body will become lifeless, because I am its life. Just so is Christ our life. That is the only reason we can live for eternity.

Has the Jew Special Advantages?

Beginning with verse 1 of Romans 3, the Apostle Paul handles the next portion of his book as one would expect an attorney to handle the questions of his clients. Certain arguments are presented in answer to some very specific questions.

The first question is raised in verse 1. In essence it asked: "What is the use of being a Jew? Has he no advantages over the Gentile? Has not God made a particular people out of

44

Israel?" The answer, of course, is that they have had certain advantages. To the Jew was given the Word of God. God spoke to the nation of Israel and through it to the Gentiles. But because Israel as a nation turned away from God, He then gave certain blessings to the Gentiles. This is where you and I came into the picture.

Is God Unfaithful?

The second question is raised in verse 3 where we read, "For what if some did not believe? shall their unbelief make the faith of God without effect?" What is meant here is, does their unfaithfulness to that which God gave them, make God unfaithful to them? The Israelites had the Word of God some 1500 years before Christ came, but they rejected Christ and later rejected the testimony of Paul. It was then that Paul declared he would turn to the Gentiles. Does all this mean that God will not keep His promises to Israel?

There are some, I am sad to say, who teach that God set aside the people of Israel finally and completely, and has taken another people to Himself. Their teaching is that you and I are Israel. That teaching does not come from the Word of God. God is not unfaithful. He cannot and will not deny Himself, for that is what He would be doing if He broke His promises to Israel. In II Timothy 2:13 we find these words: "If we believe not [if we are not faithful], yet he [God] abideth faithful: he cannot deny himself." In chapters 9, 10 and 11 of the Book of Romans God shows how He has dealt with Israel in the past, how He is dealing with them at the present, and how He will deal with them again in the future. He has not cast them off forever. They are not forgotten. Here is what he says about Israel's present condition: "For I would not, brethren, that ye should be ignorant of this mystery, lest ye should be wise in your own conceits; that blindness in part is happened to Israel, until the fulness of the Gentiles be come in" (Rom. 11:25). God is not through with His ancient people. As soon as He has finished His earthly program with the Church, He will take up His dealings with Israel again.

Is God Unrighteous?

Still a third question is raised: "But if our unrighteousness commend the righteousness of God, what shall we say? Is God unrighteous who taketh vengeance? (I speak as a man) God forbid: for then how shall God judge the world?" (vv. 5,6). The argument presented may be restated in this way: "If our unfaithfulness has made it possible for God's glory to reach out to multitudes of others, particularly the Gentiles, would it not be better for us who are Jews to keep on being unfaithful so that God's glory could keep on reaching out?" But that does not end the argument. The last part could be said thus: "If the unfaithfulness of us Jews means glory to God with more souls going to heaven, then our unfaithfulness has actually been to God's advantage."

What a diabolical argument that is. Such reasoning would mean that a lie makes the truth stand out more, and for that reason should be excused. "Why punish a liar since his lie makes the truth so prominent? But for the lie we might not have thought of the truth." And so it goes on to its logical conclusion, asking why men do not continue doing evil in order that good might come, for does not the presence of evil accentuate the grace of God?

There are persons who accuse us of that very thing. Because we believe the Bible teaches that a person who trusts in Christ receives eternal life and is secure in the Saviour, some say we believe men may live as they please. That is no real argument against the truth; and furthermore, God punishes sin. He is not glorified in our sinning; His glory is seen in providing the remedy for sin. God maintains strict discipline with His children, and sin brings His chastisement.

Sin, though black as night, can be utterly removed by the grace of God. This exalts God's grace, but it does not give a reason for men continuing in sin.

Memory Assignment:
Memorize Colossians 2:6.

EXAMINATION

In the blank spaces at the right-hand margin write the letter of the correct or most nearly correct answer.

1. Because God has demonstrated His power on behalf of the Jewish people:
   (a) the Jewish people will be saved whether they believe in Christ or not
   (b) God will not frustrate His grace by punishing Israel
   (c) individuals of that nation who turned away from faith in Christ will face greater condemnation   _____

2. Christians whose lives are not consistent with what they profess:
   (a) can often deceive everyone
   (b) will cause God's name to be blasphemed among unbelievers
   (c) will cause the unsaved to want to become Christians

   _____

3. When people have only mere religion:
   (a) they are at least a good influence upon those around them
   (b) they can be sure of pleasing God to some extent
   (c) their religion does them no good, and may do others great harm   _____

4. What God requires is:
   (a) a religious life that will match the standards of one's church
   (b) a heart attitude toward Him that will govern all parts of one's life
   (c) a heart attitude of "doing unto others as you would want them to do to you"   _____

5. Cleansing, forgiveness and a new holy life are available to all:
   (a) who can live up to God's requirements
   (b) who can understand the teachings of Scripture
   (c) who will simply receive Jesus Christ as Saviour

   _____

Complete the following:

6. God proved to the Jews that they had _____ in what they were seeking to do outwardly.

7. When Christ comes into one's life He does His work first _____ and then shows evidence of it outwardly.

8. Christ is Himself the _____ of the believer.

9. One of the advantages of the Jewish race was that through them God gave His _____.

10. Because Israel turned away from God, He gave certain blessings to the _____.

In the right-hand margin write "True" or "False" after each of the following statements:

11. Israel's rejection of God's Son cancelled God's promise to that nation. _____

12. Believers of today have replaced Israel in God's program for the world. _____

13. As soon as God has finished with His earthly program for the Church, He will take up His dealings with Israel again. _____

14. Man's sinning is less serious if others benefit from it. _____

15. Sin, regardless of its degree, can be utterly removed by the grace of God. _____

☐ **I have memorized Colossians 2:6.**

unit 6

The Whole World Guilty Before God

With Romans 3:9, we come to a new division in the book. Here God gives His final verdict concerning the human race and finds the whole world guilty before Him.

We have already seen that the heathen or Gentiles stand condemned before God, having rejected Him and having substituted false gods in His place. In chapter 2 we saw the moral man who comes far short of what God requires when he is measured by God's standards. Though he boasts of his morality, the moral man is guilty before God. Then we saw the religious man, the Jew (and that could apply to the religious Gentile as well) who had the Word of God. He, too, is condemned because he has turned away from it.

In this section, which continues through verse 20, God proves that all mankind is in a state of spiritual corruption. There is first the divine indictment against all mankind; second, the divine diagnosis of man's spiritual condition; and finally, a divine summary of man's total guilt and condemnation and utter helplessness before God.

God's Indictment of Man

In verse 9 Paul asks: "What then? are we better than they? No, in no wise: for we have before proved both Jews and Gentiles, that they are all under sin." Similar to this is the statement in verse 23 which reads: "For all have sinned, and come short of the glory of God." That is, men have come short of attaining to or earning that which would provide them with salvation. Their condition is such that they are "all under sin." Sin is pictured here as a tyrant who holds captive all men and enslaves them everywhere. The indictment is universal. There are no exceptions.

God's Diagnosis of Man's Spiritual State

Beginning with verse 10 God gives us the divine diagnosis of man's spiritual condition. He says, "As it is written, There is none righteous, no, not one." The words "all" and "not" are significant in this section. They are used over and over again to describe the universality of man's fallen condition. This is not my writing. This is not even Paul's writing though he was the human author of the Book of Romans. This is not what the Church wrote. This diagnosis is not the diagnosis of some sect or branch of Christians. This is God speaking. The Holy Spirit caused these words to be penned for us. It is God who has diagnosed man's spiritual condition, and He says there is "none righteous, no, not one."

Man is evil and totally depraved at heart. No one can produce the righteousness that God requires. Men can produce a righteousness that will meet their own low standards but we are dealing here with God's standards. It is from this standpoint that God says there is none righteous.

The passage continues, "There is none that understandeth, there is none that seeketh after God" (v. 11). Men are not only ignorant of spiritual realities, they do not even seek them. But neither would men know spiritual realities if they found them. In I Corinthians 2:14 Paul wrote, "But the natural man receiveth not the things of the Spirit of God: for they are foolishness unto him: neither can he know them, because they are spiritually discerned." The unsaved man can never understand the things of God. He may think he has some understanding of these matters, but God's verdict is that he does not.

I have heard some persons say over and over again that they do not see why God would be so hard on men. Why does God condemn a man for just one sin? In our natural state we will never understand God's spiritual standards. Men, though they have an innate consciousness of God, do not seek Him. Man's quest is not for spiritual things but for material and temporal things.

God is not through with His diagnosis, for He says, "They are all gone out of the way" (v. 12). Mankind has become side-tracked. Men walk in their own ways and not in God's way. The Lord Jesus said, "I am the way, the truth, and the life: no man cometh unto the Father, but by me." We must accept God's verdict in this. It is with Him we have to deal. It is His heaven we want to inherit. It is in His dwelling place we want to live. In order to do so, we must turn from our own way to God's way.

God further says, "They are together become unprofitable." Man was created to serve and to glorify God. But universally man is unprofitable to Him. Some may be profitable to their church, but that in itself does not make them profitable to God. The natural man is outside of God, not born again, and is not fulfilling God's purpose. Men by themselves are incapable of doing good according to the standard of goodness that God raises. Man is unrighteous in his nature. He is depraved. Everything he does is tainted with sin because he is at heart a sinner.

Think of Cornelius. God said that his alms had come before Him and He recognized him. But such good works were not sufficient for Cornelius to be accepted before God. He was instructed to send for Peter who would tell him what he must do to be saved. That is why there must be messengers of the cross. That is why there is such an organization as the Back to the Bible Broadcast. It is part of our obligation to tell men that nothing they do will merit salvation. Only Christ can save.

The Tongue

In the next several verses God shows how that in every way man expresses himself he does evil and not good and is unprofitable instead of profitable.

God begins with man's tongue. "Their throat is an open sepulchre; with their tongues they have used deceit; the poison of asps is under their lips: Whose mouth is full of cursing and bitterness" (vv. 13,14). Man's tongue (his speech) indicates the condition of his heart. Our Saviour said in Matthew 15:18,19: "But those things which proceed out of the mouth come forth from the heart; and they defile the man. For out of the heart proceed evil thoughts, murders, adulteries, fornications, thefts, false witness, blasphemies." These are the things that defile a man, and he expresses his thoughts and his intentions through his tongue.

The tongue is like a valve that erupts under pressure, and the resulting explosion shows what is in the heart. James deals with the same truth when he says, "Even so the tongue is a little member, and boasteth great things. Behold, how great a matter a little fire kindleth!" (3:5). He also describes the tongue as a fire and a world of iniquity, telling us that it defiles the whole body and sets on fire the course of nature, having itself been set on fire of hell. Then he concludes, "But the tongue can no man tame; it is an unruly evil, full of deadly poison." This is what God says through James concerning man's tongue. As a man thinks, so he speaks.

In this section in Romans, God describes the speech of man as having four different places of origin—the throat, the tongue, the lips and the mouth. The throat is described as an open sepulchre depicting unspeakable corruption (v. 13). Note how the conversation of the average unregenerate man can be repulsive to us; how much more abhorrent must it be to God who cannot even think evil!

The tongue is pictured as an organ of deceit which expresses the deceitful character of the human heart. The lips disseminate poison through lies. The mouth is said to be full of cursing and bitterness. It is a cesspool of ungodliness indulging in cursing, slander and gossip. There are many Christians who have never yet been able to bring this member of their bodies under control. As small a member of the body as the tongue is, man cannot control it. But God can. He provides the way out for man. The natural man could never stand in the presence of God and be favorably received as long as his throat, tongue, lips and mouth are so terribly evil.

The Feet

Next the feet are described. God says, "Their feet are swift to shed blood: Destruction and misery are in their ways" (vv. 15,16). Sin is lawlessness, and it is this lawlessness which is responsible for many of the horrible sins being committed today. We see the eagerness with which men will shed blood in the unjust wars that have raged with their consequent destruction of life. The crime of murder is on the increase, proving again what is in the heart of the natural man. Not all men are guilty of committing murder, and not all have shed innocent blood; but it is in the nature of man to do these things—and all are capable of doing them.

No Peace

"The way of peace have they not known: There is no fear of God before their eyes," are the words God uses to climax this particular description of man's evil ways (vv. 17,18). Sinful man does not find the way of peace. In these days everything possible is being tried in order to avoid another world war. We are spending millions—even billions of dollars trying to keep peace in the world, but in spite of all that men do wars continue to flare up. The trouble is that there is no peace in the heart of the man outside of Christ.

To the believer our Saviour said, "Peace I leave with you, my peace I give unto you: not as the world giveth, give I unto you. Let not your heart be troubled, neither let it be afraid" (John 14:27). Again He said, "These things I have spoken unto you, that in me ye might have peace. In the world ye shall have tribulation: but be of good cheer; I have overcome the world" (John 16:33).

Man's basic problem—the root cause of all his trouble—is that he does not fear God. Men have taken it for granted that God will overlook what they do and will take care of them regardless of how they live. Man's refusal to make God the God of their lives is the fountain from which all these evils flow.

Memory Assignment:
Memorize Romans 3:9.

EXAMINATION

Complete the following:

1. In Romans 3:9-20 God proves that all mankind is in a state of _____ corruption.

2. God says, "All have _____, and come _____ of the glory of God."

3. Man's spiritual condition is revealed in the words, "There is _____ righteous, no, _____ _____."

4. No man can produce a righteousness which will meet _____ standards.

5. It is _____ who has diagnosed man's spiritual condition, and Who says there is none righteous.

In the blank space at the right-hand margin write the letter of the correct or most nearly correct answer.

6. When the Scripture says, "There is none that understandeth," it means:
   (a) the way of salvation is hard to understand
   (b) no man can understand the ways of God
   (c) men are ignorant of spiritual realities   _____

7. Which of the following verses is from the Book of Romans?
   (a) "They are all gone out of the way."
   (b) "No man cometh unto the Father, but by me."
   (c) "All we like sheep have gone astray."   _____

8. When God says, "They are together become unprofitable," He means:
   (a) the natural man is unprofitable to his church
   (b) all men are worthless in God's sight
   (c) the natural man is not fulfilling God's purpose   _____

9. The true condition of a man's heart is shown by:
   (a) his speech
   (b) his actions
   (c) the friends he chooses   _____

10. Many Christians continue to lie and gossip because:
    (a) it is impossible to control the tongue
    (b) they have not allowed God to control their tongues
    (c) the quality of a Christian's speech is not important, since his sins have already been forgiven _____

In the right-hand margin write "True" or "False" after each of the following statements:

11. The statement, "Their feet are swift to shed blood," refers to men's eagerness for war. _____

12. Not everyone has a nature which is capable of committing murder. _____

13. Peace of heart can be obtained by religious experiences. _____

14. Jesus indicated that His followers could find peace on the basis of His words. _____

15. The root cause of all of man's trouble is that he does not understand himself. _____

☐ **I have memorized Romans 3:9.**

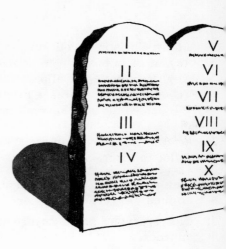

unit 7

Mankind Stands Condemned

The conclusion of Romans 3:9-20 is reached in verses 19 and 20 where God declares man to be totally condemned. "Now we know that what things soever the law saith, it saith to them who are under the law: that every mouth may be stopped, and all the world may become guilty before God. Therefore by the deeds of the law there shall no flesh be justified in his sight: for by the law is the knowledge of sin." The law, contrary to the opinion of many, condemns all men. It is surprising how many people believe that by keeping the law they can be saved; but this kind of thinking is Satan's doing. He loves nothing better than to take a verse out of its context and make it mean something other than what it says. He is pleased if he can get people to become complacent concerning their eternal welfare, lulling them into a state of passivity until they die and find themselves doomed to hell—eternally lost.

The Holiness of the Law

Those who want to place themselves under the law for salvation ought to consider what the law actually does. In verse 19 we see that it stops every mouth and causes men to stand before God without excuse for what they have done. It does not bring life but condemnation.

Consider for a moment the high standards of the law. It says, "Thou shalt love the Lord thy God with all thy heart, and with all thy soul, and with all thy strength, and with all thy mind; and thy neighbour as thyself" (Luke 10:27). Carefully analyze this statement. God says this is what the law requires men should do, not just for a moment but all the time. The whole love of man's soulish life is to be centered in God. He is never to put his own interests ahead of God. Loving God means thinking only of His good and not one's own. The mind is to be set on thinking only of what will benefit Him; every bit of strength is to be used in pleasing Him.

The law also tells us that we are to love our neighbors as ourselves. Those things that we might normally want for ourselves, we should want for our neighbors instead. Right away some will exclaim: "Well, who does that?" That is the point exactly. Who lives this way?

Where do we stand in the sight of God? God's holiness is absolute. There is not one iota, not one tiny speck of wrong in God. He is holy through and through. Furthermore, He never can and never will lower His standard of righteousness below what He himself is. If He were to do so, He would not be God. We excuse this wrong thing or that wrong thing but sin is sin to God. He will not pass over any deviation from His standards.

Not long after God had delivered the Israelites from Egypt they began to murmur against Him and lived displeasing to Him. He gave them His law which set before them His righteous standards; and the method He employed for the discipline of His people showed how fully He was against sin. They were His chosen people for whom He cared as He had never cared for any other nation. His provisions for them were daily miracles as they traveled through the desert.

When He gave the law, He came to the mountain, but the people stood apart from it. This is what the people saw: "And it came to pass on the third day in the morning, that there were thunders and lightnings, and a thick cloud upon the mount, and the voice of the trumpet exceeding loud; so that all the people that was in the camp trembled. . . . And mount Sinai was altogether on a smoke, because the Lord descended upon it in fire: and the smoke thereof ascended as the smoke of a furnace, and the whole mount quaked greatly" (Ex. 19:16-18). Why all these terrifying and dreadful signs? Because the holy God was drawing near to that which was sinful on the earth. As He came near to the presence of sin in His people, He manifested condemnation and judgment against their character and behavior.

This awe-inspiring sight was understood by the Israelites: "And all the people saw the thunderings, and the lightnings, and the noise of the trumpet, and the mountain smoking: and when the people saw it, they removed, and stood afar off. And they said unto Moses, Speak thou with us, and we will hear: but let not God speak with us, lest we die" (Ex. 20:18,19). This impressed them with the righteousness of God as possibly nothing else could. They realized that if God spoke to them directly in His holiness they could not live.

When the Lord Jesus Christ hung upon the cross bearing our sins, God turned His face from Him. There came a terrible darkness and an earthquake of such magnitude as was possibly not known in that area before. Why? Because God was speaking in holiness.

In the light of these facts, a person who would put himself under law should know what the law says, what it stands for, and the holiness of God who gave it. Those who claim that law keeping is for salvation, neither know God nor their own sinful selves.

The Purpose of the Law

This passage in Romans 3 also tells us the purpose of the law. It tells us what the law cannot do, then it tells us what the law does. Looking at the questions from the negative side we see that the law does not justify. Justification is an act of God's free grace whereby He pardons our sins and declares us to be righteous in His sight. His pardon covers sin: past, present and future. This covers all sin regardless of whether it is sins of omission, sins of commission, or even sins of thought. It includes many things we do not even recognize as sin. He pardoned them all.

Secondly, He receives us into His presence as those who have a righteousness equal to His own. We are looked upon as being as holy as He is. Such, however, the law cannot do. It cannot pardon, neither can it declare a man righteous.

Look at the matter in another way for a moment. Here, let us say, is a man who has committed a crime, and has been caught and placed in the penitentiary. The law has spoken and has found him guilty of breaking the penal code. For this he is condemned and placed behind prison bars. But he protests, saying, "I am going straight from now on." And he does. He proves it by his changed conduct. But does his conduct in the prison atone for his past crime? Does that warrant pardon for the crime he committed? Absolutely not! Even though from the moment he was caught and condemned, he started to reform, that could not set the past right. Could he demand release on the basis of his new resolution? Not even human courts handle crime in that way.

The same is true with respect to the things of God. Even if it were possible for a man to make and keep a resolution that from a certain point in his life he would no longer disobey God, still the past would not be atoned for by the good he would do.

The law cannot justify. How clearly this is expressed in Galatians 3:21: "For if there had been a law given which could have given life verily righteousness should have been by the law." This same truth is stated in Galatians 2:16: "Knowing that a man is not justified by the works of the law, but by the faith of Jesus Christ, even we have believed in Jesus Christ, that we might be justified by the faith of Christ, and not by the works of the law: for by the works of the law shall no flesh be justified."

But some may want to argue and say that if a man did live up to the law would he not be justified? God does not approach the subject from that angle for one very good reason: man does not, and cannot, live up to the law. He would have to live up to it from the moment he was born until the day he died and never deviate from it in even one point. What then is the purpose of the law? The answer is clear: "By the law is the knowledge of sin."

The law is a moral mirror produced by God. It is a mirror reflecting God's absolute holiness. It is held up for men to look into so that they might see themselves for what they really are. The law was never given for men to keep in order to be saved. It was given as a mirror to reflect the holiness of God so that man, seeing his own imperfection in that glorious light, would turn to Christ for salvation.

Read again from Galatians: "Wherefore then serveth the law? It was added because of transgressions, till the seed should come to whom the promise was made; and it was ordained by angels in the hand of a mediator" (Gal. 3:19). The law was added not because the people were good, but because they were sinning against God. They did not realize, however, that they were sinning. The law was given to impress that fact upon them.

It is as if God said to them, "Here, look into this mirror and see what sin really is. See for yourself what you are and recognize that you are sinners." In Galatians again we read, "Wherefore the law was our schoolmaster to bring us unto Christ, that we might be justified by faith. But after that faith is come, we are no longer under a schoolmaster" (Gal. 3:24).

The same truth is brought out clearly in Romans chapter 7, where Paul says, "What shall we say then? Is the law sin? God forbid. Nay, I had not known sin, but by the law: for I had not known lust, except the law had said, Thou shalt not covet." There can be no mistaking the purpose of the law. It was given to reveal our sinfulness to us.

Memory Assignment:
Memorize Romans 3:20.

EXAMINATION

Complete the following:

1. The Scripture declares (Rom. 3:20), "By the deeds of the law shall _____ _____ be justified in his [God's] sight."

2. _____ is the author of the idea that the law condemns all men.

3. Those who remain complacent about their eternal welfare will finally find themselves eternally _____.

4. The law leaves men without _____ before God.

5. The law says that man's love is to be basically centered upon _____.

In the blank space at the right-hand margin write the letter of the correct or most nearly correct answer.

6. God's standard of righteousness:
   - (a) is more lenient in the Christian era than it was in Old Testament times
   - (b) remains absolute in accord with His holiness
   - (c) varies for each person according to his knowledge of right and wrong   _____

7. In God's judgment of man's sin:
   - (a) He will not punish a sinner who has been sincere in his beliefs
   - (b) He cannot pass over any deviations from His standard
   - (c) He will understand and will give rewards according to His love and mercy   _____

8. The reason for the terrifying signs of smoke, fire and quaking of the ground when God gave the law at Mount Sinai showed that:
   (a) God was expressing displeasure with His people
   (b) a holy God was drawing near to a sinful people
   (c) God desired to frighten His people _____

9. The reason for the darkness and earthquake at the crucifixion of Christ was:
   (a) it was a coincidence of nature
   (b) God was showing His displeasure with men for killing His Son
   (c) God was showing His holiness in turning away from the sin of the world being borne by Christ on the cross _____

10. Those who claim that lawkeeping is for salvation:
   (a) neither know God nor their own sinful lives
   (b) are correctly interpreting the Scriptures
   (c) have the best possible motivation for holy living _____

In the right-hand margin write "True" or "False" after each of the following statements:

11. The fact that no one can be justified by the works of the law is plainly taught in the New Testament Book of Galatians. _____

12. God does not even offer justification for living up to the law because no man does, or can, live up to the law. _____

13. The basic aim of the law was to help men earn their salvation. _____

14. The law is like a mirror reflecting God's holiness. _____

15. The purpose of the law is to give a knowledge of sin. _____

☐ I have memorized Romans 3:20.

unit 8

God's Method of Redemption

The very heart of the gospel is presented to us in Romans 3:21-31. The section begins: "But now the righteousness of God without the law is manifested, being witnessed by the law and the prophets; Even the righteousness of God which is by faith of Jesus Christ unto all and upon all them that believe: for there is no difference: For all have sinned, and come short of the glory of God; Being justified freely by his grace through the redemption that is in Christ Jesus" (vv. 21-24).

A Time Element

How very significant are the words: "But now." The word "now" has a time element in it. It reminds us of the first chapter of John's Gospel where we read: "For the law was given by Moses, but grace and truth came by Jesus Christ." Grace is always in contrast to the law. Grace is God's kindness and love in Christ on the basis of which He gives righteousness to men. The law on the other hand demands righteousness which man in himself cannot supply. The law is connected with Moses and works; grace is connected with Christ and faith. The law blesses the good, but grace saves the bad. The law demands that blessings be earned, whereas grace is the free gift of God. Our Romans passage shows us that the relationship which grace alone can establish has been made possible through Christ.

The word "righteousness" can be interpreted to mean that standing in grace which man has before God through faith in Christ. By means of this "right standing" we come into the presence of God. This righteousness is imputed to us in Christ.

It is not a righteousness God demands in our everyday walk before He will save us. This is a righteousness apart from all works.

It was of this righteousness Paul wrote in Romans 1:16,17 when he said, "For I am not ashamed of the gospel of Christ: for it is the power of God unto salvation to every one that believeth; to the Jew first, and also to the Greek. For therein is the righteousness of God revealed." God's righteousness is revealed in the gospel, and it is revealed in order that it might be given to man.

This righteousness has to do with our right standing before God. It is a righteousness which is Christ himself, for I Corinthians 1:30 says, "But of him are ye in Christ Jesus, who of God is made unto us . . . righteousness." That which God counts righteousness is now put to our account.

What we could not do Christ did. He himself fully met every demand of the law, and His right standing before God is now put to our account. We who stand guilty before the law both as to our nature and our conduct are, through the righteousness provided in Christ, acquitted from guilt and made to stand before God clothed in Christ's righteousness.

A Necessary Distinction

This righteousness does not come as a result of our obedience and good living. Paul wrote these words to the Philippians: "That I might be found in him, not having mine own righteousness" (Phil. 3:9). Paul well knew that he could not stand before God on the basis of righteousness obtained in his daily life. Only the righteousness which is through faith in Christ, and which is imputed to us by God, can suffice here.

Look at this in another way, for it is something we must clearly understand. We know that we must be born into God's family. When we are born into His family He works in our lives to produce righteous living in us through faith. That, however, is what some have called imparted righteousness, and that in turn has to do with our state or walk on the earth. But if that were all the righteousness we had, it would not be sufficient. The moment we did something wrong we would feel condemned and possibly in despair, for Satan would take us back to the law again and insist that we obey it rather than trusting in Jesus

Christ. We need a righteousness that is absolute and established so that it cannot be changed. It is this righteousness that God gives us the moment we believe. Consequently, even though our daily life may fluctuate our right standing before God is never changed. We have a position in heaven before God in the Lord Jesus Christ. This remains unchanged, though our daily walk is not always the same.

It is this right standing before God that gives us salvation from the guilt of sin. It is through this that we have eternal life. This is a righteousness which He puts to our account now. The second aspect of righteousness which is made possible through the Holy Spirit is not something that adds to our righteous standing which we have now in Christ. It will never make us more saved. We are perfectly righteous in Christ and that perfection cannot be improved on.

This righteousness of God in Christ is not something new, for it was testified of by the law and the prophets in the Old Testament. It becomes the possession of anyone who will trust, believe, receive Jesus Christ as personal Saviour. This is God's divine method of working. This truth is not confined to the Book of Romans. In II Corinthians 5:21 Paul says, "For he hath made him [Christ] to be sin for us [taking our place, acting as our substitute], who knew no sin; that we might be made the righteousness of God in him."

God makes no distinction among men in this matter. There is first of all no difference in us, for all have committed sin. None of us by nature attain to the glory of God, we all come far behind. We have been found in sin in three different ways: we commit acts of sin; we are wrong in our nature; and we live in sin. It is utterly impossible for us under such conditions to save ourselves; only God through an act of love and grace can do that. It is for this reason the Scripture says that we are "justified freely by his grace." Salvation is by no other method.

The Ground of Justification

The Book of Romans presents its subject matter somewhat as an attorney would do in a courtroom, giving a reasonable answer to the questions raised. In the light of the material already covered, a most thoughtful and reasonable question would be, "Upon what grounds can God justify a sinner? Will He do it by overlooking sin?" If He did, He would have to overlook sin for everybody. Romans 3:25 tells us what actually is God's means of justifying a sinner. The verse reads, "Whom God hath set forth to be a propitiation through faith in his blood, to declare his righteousness for the remission of sins that are past, through the forbearance of God."

We have already seen from our study in Romans that whatever God does for one, He has to do for all, because all are equally lost. There is no difference in men, for all have sinned and come short of God's glory. One may argue that some have come closer to God's standards than others, but that still does not change the picture—all have fallen short. By way of illustration, consider the bridging of the Grand Canyon. In places it is some 15 miles across. Suppose someone built a bridge that would span 5 miles—it would come far short of bridging the canyon. Someone else might build another bridge 14 miles long, but it would also come short of bridging the canyon.

All of us have come short of God's glory and are hopelessly doomed apart from His stepping in and providing, through grace, a way of escape for us. And the method He uses is the same for all—redemption through Christ Jesus.

We are all under sin according to the Scriptures. And as Paul says in Romans 6:23: "The wages of sin is death." We need to be redeemed from sin. If the wages of sin is death, then the purchase price must be something connected with death, so we read in Romans 5:8: "But God commendeth his love toward us, in that, while we were yet sinners, Christ died for us."

The Lord Jesus became the sinner in our place. He made this very plain in the days of His public ministry when He said, "Even as the Son of man came not to be ministered unto, but to minister, and to give his life a ransom for many" (Matt. 20:28). The purchase price of sin is the precious blood of Jesus Christ who died, not for His own sin, for He had no sin, but for our sin.

We have already seen that redemption goes beyond emancipation from the guilt of sin. It includes deliverance from the power of sin also. This was illustrated for us in Israel's experience when they were first delivered by blood from the death angel in Egypt, and then delivered by power at the Red Sea. The redemption by power is taken up in chapters 6, 7 and 8 of Romans.

Let us take a closer look at God's method of declaring men righteous.

Christ, we are told, has been set forth by God to be a propitiation through faith in His blood. Do not confuse this with the thought of appeasement. Jesus did not come to appease God's wrath, but through His sacrifice removed the need for God's wrath. In the sense in which we are using the word appease, God can never be appeased. We might appease Satan for a while or at least appease those who serve him on this earth, such as the Communists, but we cannot appease God. God is just and must be propitiated. Something must be done that will satisfy God regarding the penalty of sin. Our Saviour kept the law to perfection and also paid the full price of the penalty of our failure to keep the law. Christ became our propitiation before God, and by this God retained His integrity and was able to forgive sins even in Old Testament times.

There are many who are puzzled when we say that the people in Old Testament times were saved apart from law keeping, even though Christ had not yet died for them. God's plan of redemption is wonderful to contemplate. God not only foreknew our sin, but He also planned before the foundation of the world for our redemption. Jesus was to pay the price of sin and on the basis of what He would do, God retained His full integrity while yet forgiving the sins of men and women in Old Testament days. Under the law, men brought sacrifices which were not a substitute for Christ, but were shadows of His real atonement and as such were assurances of what He would do. These sacrifices provided a temporary suspension of God's judgment on sin, because they looked forward to the full redemption price which would be paid by Christ.

The Old Testament believers looked forward by faith to the work that Christ would do. The bringing of their sacrifices became the evidence of their faith with regard to that future work. Judgment was suspended until Jesus came to completely atone for their sins.

That is the wonderful thing about God and His method of salvation. He provided a way that fully propitiated Himself, but at the same time took care of judgment on sin, and provided justification for men.

There is no room for man to boast under a system of salvation like this. The law of faith leaves no room for man to boast in his own abilities as would a law of works. One of the results of this kind of salvation is humility. It makes no difference whether we are religious, moral, great, or small—all must come the same way. None can attain unto perfect righteousness or have a proper and right standing before God on the basis of works. Works are discounted entirely. Faith is the principle here. This remedy is universal for it is not only good for the Jew but also for the Gentile.

Memory Assignment:
Memorize Romans 3:22,23.

EXAMINATION

In the right-hand margin write "True" or "False" after each of the following statements:

1. Grace is always in contrast to the law. _____
2. The word "righteousness" in Romans 3 refers to the standing a man has before God because of his own goodness.

   _____
3. The righteousness which God gives is actually Christ himself. _____
4. The saved person is acquitted from guilt and stands before God clothed in Christ's righteousness. _____
5. The righteous living of a Christian produced through the Holy Spirit is sufficient to save him from the guilt of sin.

   _____

Complete the following:

6. Though the Christian's daily walk is not always the same, his position before God remains _____.
7. The Scriptures declare that we are "justified freely by his [God's] _____."
8. There is no difference among men, for all have _____ and come short of God's glory.
9. We need to be redeemed from sin because "the wages of sin is _____" (Rom. 6:23).
10. God justifies sinners on the basis that "Christ _____ for us."

In the blank space at the right-hand margin write the letter of the correct or most nearly correct answer.

11. Redemption, going beyond freedom from the guilt of sin, also includes:
    (a) deliverance from the presence of sin in daily life
    (b) deliverance from the consequences of sin in daily life
    (c) deliverance from the power of sin in daily life _____

12. The death of Jesus Christ was:
    (a) an appeasement for God's wrath
    (b) full satisfaction to God for the penalty of sin
    (c) a martyrdom for a good cause _____

13. Christ became the propitiation for our sin:
    (a) through His high moral example
    (b) through His exemplary life
    (c) through His perfect observance of the law and His death for the penalty for our sin _____

14. People in Old Testament times were saved:
    (a) through the keeping of the law
    (b) by faith and made sacrifices which looked forward to Christ's death
    (c) by making sacrifices which were full payment for their sins _____

15. Sacrifices made by people in Old Testament times:
    (a) were rituals without meaning
    (b) provided a temporary suspension of God's judgment on sin
    (c) fully satisfied God for the penalty of their sin _____

☐ **I have memorized Romans 3:22,23.**

unit 9

Justification Illustrated

How a man may have a right standing before God is clearly illustrated in the life of Abraham. This position was given to him through faith—not through works. "Abraham believed God," we are told, "and it was counted unto him for righteousness" (Rom. 4:3). Abraham's sin was put on Christ's account, and Christ paid the full price. The same truth holds for us. What we owe has been paid by Christ; our sin account was settled by Him.

Jesus is at the right hand of the Father and says to Him both as concerning Abraham and us, "Receive him as myself." On the basis of faith, every believer is received before God, not in his own rights or in his own name, but in the rights and Name of Christ.

No Contradiction

Some feel that the message in Romans 4 contradicts the one in chapter 2 of the Book of James. James 2:21-24 says: "Was not Abraham our father justified by works, when he had offered Isaac his son upon the altar? Seest thou how faith wrought with his works, and by works was faith made perfect [mature]? And the scripture was fulfilled which saith, Abraham believed God, and it was imputed unto him for righteousness: and he was called the Friend of God. Ye see then how that by works a man is justified, and not by faith only [or alone]." There is no real contradiction here. What we have are two aspects of the same truth. Paul speaks of that which justifies a man before God, for he says, "If Abraham were justified by works, he hath whereof to glory; but not before God" (Rom. 4:2). Abraham believed God, and God counted it to him for righteousness.

Consequently, this aspect of righteousness is entirely by faith and apart from works.

James, on the other hand, talks about the *proof* of justification. The man who professes to have justifying faith must prove it to men. And this, of course, he does by the life he lives. Paul speaks of that which a man has by faith, namely, justification before God. James speaks of what men see and which proves to them that a man is saved.

Paul draws an illustration from Genesis 15:6 where Abraham believed God, and God counted it to him for righteousness. James, on the other hand, took his illustration from chapter 22 of Genesis where Abraham was called upon to offer up his son, Isaac. This aspect of Abraham's life is further explained in Hebrews 11:17-19: "By faith Abraham, when he was tried, offered up Isaac: and he that had received the promises offered up his only begotten son. Of whom it was said, That in Isaac shall thy seed be called: Accounting that God was able to raise him up, even from the dead; from whence also he received him in a figure."

The faith that justifies us before God is spoken of again in Romans 4 where it is said of Abraham, "And being not weak in faith, he considered not his own body now dead, when he was about an hundred years old, neither yet the deadness of Sarah's womb: He staggered not at the promise of God through unbelief; but was strong in faith, giving glory to God; And being fully persuaded that, what he had promised, he was able also to perform. And therefore it was imputed to him for righteousness" (vv. 19-22). Then, the apostle tells us that we, too are justified on this same faith basis. Verses 23 and 24 tell us: "Now it was not written for his sake alone, that it was imputed to him; But for us also, to whom it shall be imputed, if we believe on him that raised up Jesus our Lord from the dead."

What Is Justifying Faith?

Christ is the only righteous one, and God will pronounce us righteous only as we are united with Him. That is God's simple plan for salvation by faith.

Some will protest and say, "This is too hard for me to grasp. I do not think I can be saved by any such method."

Do not let the simplicity of it be a stumbling block. God says that if we believe in Him, He will take care of our sins.

He will take care of our righteousness. He wants us to trust Him for it. Such is grace. This is where mercy and grace meet. Mercy means that God does not punish us though we deserve it; and grace means that He gives us something when we do not deserve it. In John 1:12 we are promised: "But as many as received him, to them gave he power to become the sons of God, even to them that believe on his name." The words "receive" and "believe" are used interchangeably here, showing that the faith is an active one and not a dead one. It is a faith that not only accepts a certain fact concerning Christ, but receives the living Christ into the heart for its life.

Living Faith

It is necessary to clarify this matter, for many of God's people have been puzzled over this very thing. James writes, "What doth it profit, my brethren, though a man say he hath faith, and have not works? can faith save him?" (2:14). The original language in which this verse was written adds one word which will help us here. The question at the end should read, "Can THAT faith save him?" What faith is he speaking of? A faith that has no works. These works, of course, are not flesh works but works due to the energy of the Spirit of God within us.

Continuing on this subject, James says, "Even so faith, if it hath not works, is dead, being alone." A dead faith might be likened to what we call a historical faith. A historical fact is accepted as a mere matter of head knowledge, but it does nothing for our hearts. James illustrates this in these words: "Thou believest that there is one God; thou doest well: the devils also believe, and tremble." The demons know that there is a God and that He is going to judge them. That is why they tremble. Merely to believe that God is, is not saving faith. Saving faith is an act of faith, and with respect to Christ it means that the person placing faith in Him receives Him and all that He offers in salvation for a lost sinner.

When Christ comes into our hearts, we will show it. Our faith will be active or else it will mean nothing by way of testimony to those about us.

There are those who, when asked if they are Christians, will say that they have believed the facts of the Christian faith for as long as they can remember. That could be true and yet such persons could be lost. I believed for as long as I can remember that Jesus died for my sins. I was trained that way. I lived in a home where these truths were believed and taught. But it was not until I reached the age of twenty that I received Jesus Christ as a Person into my life.

When Was Abraham Justified?

The time of Abraham's justification is very important. The subject is raised by these words: "Cometh this blessedness then upon the circumcision only, or upon the uncircumcision also? for we say that faith was reckoned to Abraham for righteousness. How was it then reckoned? when he was in circumcision, or in uncircumcision? Not in circumcision, but in uncircumcision" (vv. 9,10). The simple meaning of this is that he was reckoned righteous before he was circumcised.

The rite of circumcision was not the means of his being justified, for the passage continues: "And he received the sign of circumcision, a seal of the righteousness of the faith which he had yet being uncircumcised: that he might be the father of all them that believe, though they be not circumcised; that righteousness might be imputed unto them also: And the father of circumcision to them who are not of the circumcision only, but who also walk in the steps of that faith of our father Abraham, which he had being yet uncircumcised" (vv. 11,12).

This is as clear as language can make it. Abraham was pronounced righteous by God upon his believing.

Then, in obedience to God he was circumcised, which was an outward sign of obedience to his inward faith. This definitely shows the sequence of steps in the Christian life. First we must believe. Having believed, we then act upon that faith, not through self-produced action, but action resulting from the new life within us.

Abraham was justified before the rite of circumcision was practiced by him. He was also justified long before the law was given. In Romans 4:13,14 Paul says, "For the promise, that he should be the heir of the world, was not to Abraham, or to his seed, through the law, but through the righteousness of faith. For if they which are of the law be heirs, faith is made void, and the promise made of none effect." The law was not given until 430 years after Abraham was justified; consequently, justification had to be by faith, because there was no law given for him to keep. Justification by faith is the principle that has been operative with God throughout all generations. At no time has there been a method of salvation by law keeping.

The key verse in this whole section is verse 16. The words are, "Therefore it is of faith, that it might be by grace; to the end the promise might be sure to all the seed; not to that only which is of the law, but to that also which is of the faith of Abraham; who is the father of us all." Salvation then is by grace through faith.

Grace demands faith. Remember that God in His mercy forgave us our sins. Because of His mercy, He did not punish us according to our just deserts. God, however, could not forgive sin, by merely overlooking it. That is where grace stepped in. God in His grace provided us with what we did not deserve, namely salvation. Christ bore our punishment in death and provided for us life and forgiveness. This can only come through faith.

We do not deserve mercy or it would not be mercy. We do not deserve grace or it would no longer be grace. It would be a matter of payment for work done. If we were really to receive from God's hand for the works we have done, we would receive death. Instead, He has given mercy and grace which can come only on the basis of faith—not human effort. Human effort would have ended in our condemnation. Faith results in our salvation.

The story of Abraham's faith is a gripping one. Read it in Genesis chapters 15, 16 and 17. He was a man who believed God when God told him what He was going to do for him. Williams' translation of verse 18 says, "Abraham, building on hope in spite of hopeless circumstances had faith." God promised Abraham that his seed would be as the stars of heaven. Yet at that time Abraham was 100 years of age and his wife Sarah was 90, and they were childless. It was as humanly impossible for Abraham to bring children into the world at that age as it was for him to meet the righteous standards of God. Nevertheless, he believed what God said, and God counted it to Him for righteousness.

These things were not written merely for the purpose of giving credit to Abraham, or that we might have historical information concerning him. They were given to show God's divine truth for all ages. Abraham believed in the God of the resurrection, the God who raised up Jesus Christ from the dead. We believe with him when we trust the same Saviour. The last verse of this chapter says, "Who was delivered for our offences, and was raised again for our justification." These two great facts in the work of our Lord are essential to our justification. Christ died because of our sins. He was raised from the dead as proof of the acceptableness of His sacrifice of God. Christ's resurrection is His assurance to us that through our personal appropriation of His death and resurrection by faith, we stand justified before God.

Memory Assignment:
Memorize Romans 4:5.

EXAMINATION

In the blank space at the right-hand margin write the letter of the correct or most nearly correct answer.

1. On the basis of faith, every believer is received before God:
   (a) according to the works he has done as a Christian
   (b) in his own rights and own name
   (c) in the rights and Name of Christ   _____

2. In speaking of faith in Romans 4, Paul refers to:
   (a) justification before God
   (b) the proof of justification
   (c) Abraham's unique faith   _____

3. In speaking of faith in James 2, James refers to:
   (a) justification before God by works
   (b) belief which is expressed by action
   (c) justification by faith without works   _____

4. Abraham's faith is described as confidence that God was able to perform:
   (a) what He had planned
   (b) what He had promised
   (c) what He had purposed   _____

5. God's plan of salvation may be simply described as:
   (a) God's accepting those whose good deeds outweigh their bad deeds
   (b) God's declaring righteous those who believe that He exists
   (c) God's declaring righteous those who through faith are united to Christ   _____

In the right-hand margin write "True" or "False" after each of the following statements:

6. Mercy means that God gives us something we do not deserve.   _____

7. Grace means that God does not punish us when we deserve it.   _____

8. In John 1:12 "believing" in Christ is the same as "receiving" Him.   _____

9. A historical faith is the same as a saving faith.   _____

10. Believing the facts of the Christian faith is sufficient to bring salvation.   _____

Complete the following:

11. Abraham was justified by faith _____ he observed the the rite of circumcision.

12. Abraham was justified by faith _____ God gave the law.

13. The key verse of this section is Romans 4:16, "Therefore it is of _____, that it might be by _____; to the end the promise might be sure to all the seed. . . ."

14. Two facts in the work of our Lord essential to our justification are His _____ and His _____.

15. Christ's _____ is His assurance that those who trust Him are justified before God.

☐ **I have memorized Romans 4:5.**

unit 10

The Results of Justification

Peace

The fifth chapter of Romans presents us with a number of specific things which result from our being justified. The first of these is peace with God. This is not a peace which depends upon our walk, but rather upon what Christ has done for us. Christ made peace with God through His precious blood. So then, "being justified by faith, we have peace with God" (v. 1). The Bible does not say we *ought* to have peace. It says we *have* peace with God. That is a fact to be enjoyed now.

Access

The next great result of justification is that we have access. The words are, "By whom also we have access by faith into this grace wherein we stand" (v. 2). "Access" means that we have an entrance into His grace. Grace is God giving us what we do not deserve. It is actually God giving us everything we need through Christ. "He that spared not his own Son, but delivered him up for us all, how shall he not with him also freely give us all things?" (Rom. 8:32). Our standing is in the grace to which we have constant access. When we come to receive blessings from God's hand it is not necessary on every occasion to have a new introduction or new credentials. Our relationship with God through Christ is such that we may enter His presence at any time.

We learn from II Corinthians 9:8 that "God is able to make all grace abound toward you; that ye, always having all sufficiency in all things, may abound to every good work."

We stand on this grace. We begin our Christian lives in it. We continue drinking from it as though it were a river that follows us wherever we go. There is a spiritual river of life flowing from the Throne of God past our heart's door at all times. All we need to do is drink.

Israel's experiences in the wilderness will help us to see this. On more than one occasion water gushed forth from the Rock to save them from dying of thirst. Paul tells us in I Corinthians 10 that the Rock which followed them was Christ. There was the actual miracle of God bringing water from a rock for Israel. This incident speaks to us of the spiritual rock of refreshment with its water of grace gushing forth for us to use on our journey.

The purpose of such a supply is not that we are to wear ourselves out trying to do what is pleasing to God, then when exhausted come to Him for refreshment. Rather, we are to start out refreshed by Him and we are to keep constantly filled by His grace and His love and His compassion. We can always depend on God to supply our every need.

Assurance of God's Presence

In addition to this standing in grace, we rejoice in the hope of the glorious gospel of Christ. It is the glory of God's presence with us that is meant here. We are one in Christ and we will never be alone again. There may be times when we feel alone, but He is with us. His promise says, "I will never leave thee nor forsake thee." We can never get out of His presence or out of His sight. We are assured of the glory of the presence of God at all times.

Read what the Psalmist had to say on this subject in Psalm 139: "O Lord, thou hast searched me, and known me. Thou knowest my downsitting and mine uprising, thou understandest my thought afar off. Thou compassest my path and my lying down, and art acquainted with all my ways. For there is not a word in my tongue, but, lo, O Lord, thou knowest it altogether. Thou hast beset me behind and before, and laid thine hand upon me. Such knowledge is too wonderful for me; it is high, I cannot attain unto it. . . . Whither shall I flee from thy presence?" (vv. 1-7).

Glory in Tribulation

Another result of our justification is that we glory in tribulation. If we will look at our trials and troubles in the right way they will take on an entirely different meaning. We not only hope in future joys which will replace the tribulations of this life, but we find we can be full of joy right here and now during the times of our trials. It is a matter of having the right attitude toward God and His dealing with us, so that patience and endurance develop mature Christian character in us and form a habit of hope within us.

True believers desire more patience and greater maturity of Christian character than they have. They want to be conscious of God's presence at all times and to have an attitude of hope under all circumstances. But how can that be brought about? Paul says that tribulation works these things for us. It is the very troubles we sometimes resent and seek to avoid that God uses to bring patience and experience and hope.

Love

Still another result of justification is that hope does not make us ashamed because the love of God has been shed abroad in our hearts by the Holy Ghost which is given unto us (v. 5). Due to the loose way in which the word "love" is used these days and the very fact that even in the Bible different words are translated by the word "love," we need to define what kind of love is meant here. The word translated "love" in this passage is not speaking primarily of an affectionate, reciprocal type of love. It is not, at its source, human love at all. It is divine love which is greater than filial love or the love of parents for their children. It is a divine love which does not require a love response from the one being loved.

This is a love which comes only from God and leads one to give himself completely for the benefit of someone else. It is that love that causes us to love our neighbor as ourselves. Human love will cause us to do everything possible for ourselves if we are ill, or to acquire something if we desire it, because we love ourselves so much. But it does not cause us to love our neighbor to that degree. It takes a higher kind of love to do that.

We are also told in Romans 5:5 that as the result of our being saved, the love of God has been shed abroad in our hearts. Human love will cause one who is loved to respond to that love; but the love of God causes one to give himself for someone who does not love in return. See how God loved: "But God commendeth his love toward us, in that, while we were yet sinners, Christ died for us" (v. 8). It is this love that is shed abroad in our hearts by the Holy Spirit.

This is not a love that we beg God for. It is something that we already have. We are to reckon it ours, count its presence in us as a fact, and act upon that fact.

How do we experience this love? It is not experienced necessarily by having a feeling or by showing affection. If we wait for some kind of an affectionate feeling for sinners before we tell them of Christ, we may never tell them. To realize, however, that they are going to hell because they are doomed without the Saviour will cause us to want to share what we have with them. We must appropriate this love by faith. It is God who works in us both to will and to do of His good pleasure. But we are not robots to be motivated by someone pressing a button. The Lord has given us this love, and it provides the motivation for putting ourselves completely at His disposal. Because of this love within us, we turn from the old life of surrendering our members as instruments to sin, and yield ourselves instead to God as those who are alive from the dead and our members as instruments of righteousness to God (Rom. 6:13).

Saved From Wrath

In verse 9 we see another result of justification. The words are, "Much more then, being now justified by his blood, we shall be saved from wrath through him." Remember that God's wrath is not a fit of temper. It is His unchanging attitude of opposition to sin. He separates himself from that which is not holy. The unsaved already have the wrath of God abiding on them. Such is the message of John 3:36: "He that believeth on the Son hath everlasting life: and he that believeth not the Son shall not see life; but the wrath of God abideth on him." Christ has delivered us from this wrath and it is the desire of God that all men might be delivered from it. They can be if they will turn in faith believing to Christ and find in Him their justification. Then to them, as to us all, these results of justification will become a reality.

Saved by Christ's Life

We have a statement in Romans 5:10 which seems to contradict what we ordinarily say regarding salvation. When asked how we are saved, we usually answer, "Through the death of the Lord Jesus Christ." But read what this verse says: "For if, when we were enemies, we were reconciled to God by the death of his Son, much more, being reconciled, we shall be saved by his life."

There are two aspects of salvation here that are very important for us to see. First, through the death of Jesus Christ, we are reconciled to God—brought back into relationship with Him—so that we can fellowship with Him and, secondly, of course, we will eventually have a home with Him. Then we are saved by His life. Since He lives, we live also. In Ephesians, the first aspect of our salvation is spoken of as our being redeemed through "His [Christ's] blood" or as "the forgiveness of sin." The second aspect is dealt with in this way. We are told that He has "predestinated us unto the adoption of children by Jesus Christ," meaning that God guarantees to take us through spiritual childhood to full maturity in the Saviour.

These two aspects are further seen in the 10th chapter of John. First of all, Christ stated both in verse 10: "I am come that they might have life, and that they might have it more abundantly." Then again in the same chapter, verses 27 and 28, the first aspect is stated in these words: "I give unto them eternal life; and they shall never perish." Because He has done away with sin we have this eternal life, and we shall never again see spiritual death. He carries this thought on to the second aspect, however, for in verse 27 He also says, "My sheep hear my voice, and I know them, and they follow me"; and the last half of 28: "Neither shall any man pluck them out of my hand." We have this surety in Him.

It is very important that we see this twofold aspect: by His death He secures our life; by His life He secures our daily living.

Coming back again to Romans 5 we find the first aspect stated in these words: "Much more then, being now justified by his blood, we shall be saved from wrath through him." So then, Christ's death removes the guilt of our sin. However, if we are to be the children of God and live pleasing to him, there are hindrances in our lives that must also be removed. This is taken up in chapter 6 where the subject of victory over the "old man" is brought to light: "Knowing this, that our old man is crucified with him, that the body of sin might be destroyed, that henceforth we should not serve sin" (v. 6). Christ alone has power to remove the hindrances of the Christian life. So once again we see that in the death of Christ we are separated from evil, and through His life our own lives are transformed into being pleasing to Him.

We must see then that the death of Christ procured salvation for us and that His risen life makes it effective in us. Had Jesus remained dead, we could never consider ourselves as being saved. He might have died for our sins, but we would still be miserable. Had He not delivered us from the power of sin and made His life effective in us, His would not have been a completed work. By His death He disarmed the power of Satan, but by His life we stand victorious against the powers of darkness.

The power of Christ's life is twofold. According to Romans 8:2 we are set free from the power of sin and death. To obey the sin nature is as natural to the unsaved man as it is for him to breathe. But, praise God, Christ has set us free from it and through His life He also gives us the power to produce the life or righteousness pleasing to God.

Memory Assignment:
Memorize Romans 5:1.

EXAMINATION

Complete the following:

1. "Being justified by faith, we have _____ with God."
2. Through Christ "we have _____ into this grace where-in we stand."
3. "God is able to make all _____ abound toward you."
4. God's promise is, "I will never _____ thee nor _____ thee."
5. Because a Christian is justified he can _____ in tribulation.

In the right-hand margin write "True" or "False" after each of the following statements:

6. The Christian has the hope that future joys will replace the tribulations of this life. _____
7. The Christian can expect tribulation to produce in him maturity of Christian character. _____
8. The love spoken of in Romans 5:8 means an affectionate type of love which expects a response to its expression.

   _____
9. The love of God will cause one to give himself even for someone who does not love in return. _____
10. Because God's love produces such blessing and fruit in the Christian's life all believers should continually ask God for His love. _____

In the blank space at the right-hand margin write the letter of the correct or most nearly correct answer.

11. Because God's love is within us:
    (a) we may yield ourselves to sin
    (b) we must try our best to love others
    (c) we must yield ourselves to God _____

12. To be delivered from God's wrath means:
    (a) one is no longer subject to God's acts of temper
    (b) one is no longer subject to God's judgment upon sin
    (c) one is no longer subject to God's discipline _____
13. According to Romans 5:10 we have been reconciled to God:
    (a) by the death of His Son
    (b) by Christ's life
    (c) by our faith in God _____
14. Spiritual victory and maturity are guaranteed by God for believers through:
    (a) a knowledge of God's Word
    (b) the life of Christ
    (c) a feeling of God's nearness _____
15. The power of Christ's life has set us free from sin's power and:
    (a) enables us to live without difficulties
    (b) enables us to live a life pleasing to God
    (c) grants us lives free from sin _____

☐ I have memorized Romans 5:1.

unit 11

Adam and Christ

Beginning with verse 12 of chapter 5 a contrast is made between the first Adam and the last Adam. Here we are told how sin and death came and how righteousness also came. This section does not read easily in our English Bibles, and for that reason many persons have passed over it and have not sought the rich truths in it.

The first part begins, "Wherefore, as by one man sin entered into the world, and death by sin; and so death passed upon all men, for that all have sinned: For until the law sin was in the world: but sin is not imputed when there is no law. Nevertheless death reigned from Adam to Moses, even over them that had not sinned after the similitude of Adam's transgression, who is the figure of him that was to come" (vv. 12-14).

In verse 12 we see the universality of sin and the universal consequence which is death. Sin entered into the world by one man—Adam. Sin is always spoken of in the Bible as being transmitted through man. Adam transmitted sin to his whole posterity and, as a result of sin, death followed. "For the wages of sin is death" (Rom. 6:23).

Sin is universal and guilt lies on every soul. All have sinned and death has passed upon all. Many people overlook the distinction between sin and sins, which accounts for the often repeated phrase, "Well, I am not such a great sinner." They overlook the fact that there is a sin nature within us, and as a result of that nature we commit acts of sin.

All of us were born as the seed of Adam. He became a fallen man and a sinner by nature. We inherited that nature from him.

85

Long before we knew anything about committing acts of sin, we were sinners by nature of our inheritance through Adam.

For evidence of this we only need to remind ourselves that death is universal. We see it in man, in animal life and in plant life. In the State of California there is a tree which is possibly the oldest living thing in the world today. It is considered to be some 4000 years of age—which dates it back to the time of Abraham. But that tree is dying, for death comes to every living thing upon this earth.

Death is the result of sin. When man sinned, death passed upon all men and upon all creation. Death is no respecter of persons, for the infant dies, moral people die, religious people die. The end is the same for all whether good or bad—they all die.

Death is a universal effect which has its universal cause in that all men are under sin, and sin brings death. The root sin of all this was Adam's sin. By it all were made sinners. This means that men are sinners by nature, and for that reason all are condemned alike.

A statement which has puzzled many is, "For until the law sin was in the world: but sin is not imputed when there is no law." This means that sin is not counted against a person when a law has not been given as it is when a law has been given.

This we have already seen in the second chapter of Romans: "For as many as have sinned without law shall also perish without law: and as many as have sinned in the law shall be judged by the law; For not the hearers of the law are just before God, but the doers of the law shall be justified. For when the Gentiles, which have not the law, do by nature the things contained in the law, these, having not the law, are a law unto themselves: Which shew the work of the law written in their hearts, their conscience also bearing witness, and their thoughts the mean while accusing or else excusing one another" (2:12-15). God judges man on the basis of the light given to him. By the coming in of the law, spiritual light to man was increased, which meant that he knew right from wrong in a clearer way. Under these circumstances the condemnation or judgment is even greater.

In the State of Nebraska where I live, we have a speed limit for daytime driving and another for nighttime driving. Suppose that in another state there is no specific speed given for daytime driving, the law simply stating that one is to drive in such a manner so as not to jeopardize life and property. Consequently, if I were to go into that state, I could increase my speed and still not be called a law breaker. That does not mean, however, that if I were to travel at a hundred miles an hour that I would not be stopped and possibly fined. Why? I would not have broken the law in the sense of having exceeded a certain speed, but I could be apprehended on the basis of jeopardizing the lives of others. The point is, that with the difference in laws in the two states I could be judged on different grounds, depending upon the nature and speed of my driving.

God's standards are not man's standards, and what men may permit may be prohibited by God—and often is. For example, there are some states in the United States where gambling is legalized. In most states it is not. Now, that does not mean that if I were to gamble in a state where gambling is legalized, I would not be doing anything wrong. So far as the laws of that state are concerned, I would not be breaking the law; but so far as the standards of God are concerned, I would be breaking His standards. Gambling is morally wrong whether done with the sanction of man's law or not.

God's law was given to expose sin and to make sin stand out as being exceedingly sinful. Men had reached the place where they were denying sin as being sin, so God gave them a law which exposed sin in its true colors. And so, as we have pointed out before, God judges men according to the light they have. Without Christ, they all stand condemned, but those who have sinned against greater light will have a greater degree of punishment.

Adam sinned against a specific commandment, for we read, "Nevertheless death reigned from Adam to Moses, even over them that had not sinned after the similitude of Adam's transgression." God had said to Adam, "The day thou eatest thereof, thou shalt surely die," speaking of the fruit of the Tree of the Knowledge of Good and Evil. Adam sinned against this specific command.

However, from the time of Adam until Moses, the lawgiver, there were no such specific commandments, nevertheless, death reigned. Why? The reason is that men were sinners by nature and sinned even though it was against less light perhaps than Adam had.

Offence and Obedience

In Romans 5:15-19, there is a detailed contrast between Adam and Christ. The result of Adam's sin is compared with Christ's obedience and righteousness. Through the offence of Adam came death, but because of the grace of Jesus Christ salvation is provided so that there is no excuse whatsoever for any man not to be reconciled to God. No man will be able to challenge God and say that God was unrighteous in His dealings with him. Over against the sin of one man is put the obedience of the other man, "For if by one man's offence death reigned by one; much more they which received abundance of grace and of the gift of righteousness shall reign in life by one, Jesus Christ." That gift is none other than Christ himself. He is the righteous one who is our eternal life.

In the closing verses of chapter 5 Paul again speaks of the law and points out that "the law entered, that the offence might abound." The law puts its finger on the spot and points out sin to be sin. A child might run into the home and the mother say to him, "Go and wash your face, for it is dirty." The child might argue that his face is not dirty, but all the mother would need to do would be to pick him up and hold him in front of a mirror. The mirror would tell the story. So it is with the law.

But the message does not end here, for we learn: "Where sin abounded, grace did much more abound." Sin is made to stand out because of the law, but that very standing out of sin adds lustre to the grace of God which is by one man, Jesus Christ. This is for us; this is for all. God's grace is absolutely sufficient for every sin.

Men are sinners by birth and practice. In chapter 5 of Romans Paul says, "Wherefore, as by one man sin entered into the world, and death by sin; and so death passed upon all men, for that all have sinned." Sin is universal and man's history bears out the apostle's words (Rom. 1:18-32). Sin must be judged by God and his judgments are right (Rom. 2:1-29). But God does not delight in judgment; His delight is in saving the sinner from his sin and the consequences of it (Rom. 3:9-31). Through Jesus Christ, God has provided a way whereby man, evil though he is by nature and practice, may stand before Him clothed in the righteousness of Jesus Christ (Rom. 3:21-26).

However, when a man is justified before God, this does not

exhaust all that God does for him. Salvation is the great inclusive word of the gospel and includes, to mention only a few, the forgiveness of sins, being declared righteous before God, receiving the new birth and the new life in Christ, and finally the redemption of the body. It is no wonder that as Paul contemplated the great sweep of salvation, he declared: "I am not ashamed of the gospel of Christ: for it is the power of God unto salvation to every one that believeth; to the Jew first, and also to the Greek" (Rom. 1:16).

The first five chapters of Romans not only show that salvation is needed and provided, but towards the last part of the fifth chapter, the ground work is laid for the subject of the victorious life in Christ. Adam bequeathed to his posterity a sin nature and death. Christ, on the other hand, through grace provides life and deliverance from the sin nature, and victorious living. "For if by one man's offence death reigned by one; much more they which receive abundance of grace and of the gift of righteousness shall reign in life by one, Jesus Christ" (5:17). Up to the time of our salvation we were under the domination of the fallen nature. But when Christ saved us and became our life in us, He made it possible for a new kind of behavior, a new kind of practice, on our part. How that victory over sin is to be achieved, and how our daily walk may be made pleasing to God is the subject of Romans 6, 7 and 8.

Memory Assignment:
Memorize Romans 5:17.

EXAMINATION

Complete the following:

1. In Romans 5 we read of the contrast between _____ and _____.
2. When Adam sinned, sin became the nature of _____ men.
3. "Sin" refers to our sinful _____, while "sins" refer to our sinful _____.
4. When man sinned, _____ passed upon all men.
5. "Sin is not imputed where there is no _____."

In the blank space at the right-hand margin write the letter of the correct or most nearly correct answer.

6. God judges man on the basis of:
   (a) the light given to him
   (b) the sincerity of his heart
   (c) the standards of his society   _____
7. God's standards and man's standards are:
   (a) always the same
   (b) always different
   (c) sometimes the same, sometimes different   _____
8. Before the law was given during the time from Adam until Moses:
   (a) men were free from God's judgment
   (b) all men faced death
   (c) men were sinless   _____
9. In the closing verses of Romans 5, Paul explains that the law entered:
   (a) that all might be condemned
   (b) that all might be saved
   (c) that man's sin might be pointed out   _____

10. The statement, "Where sin abounded, grace did much more abound," means:
    (a) great sinfulness is necessary to show the greatness of God's grace
    (b) where the law showed the greatness of sin, the sin showed the greatness of God's grace
    (c) man's sin glorifies God by showing the greatness of His grace _____

In the right-hand margin write "True" or "False" after each of the following statements:

11. Human history does not support the statement, "all have sinned." _____
12. God delights in judgment. _____
13. Salvation is a word of limited meaning. _____
14. The first five chapters of Romans show that salvation is needed and provided. _____
15. Until the time a person is saved he is under the domination of the fallen nature. _____

☐ **I have memorized Romans 5:17.**

unit 12

Rethinking Romans

The name that stands out above all others in the Book of Romans is the name "Jesus." God's redemption is through Jesus Christ for it is through Christ that we receive grace. Grace is God wanting to give man what he needs—deliverance from sin and its condemnation. No one can earn God's grace, for then it would cease to be grace. We can only receive what Christ has accomplished for us on Calvary.

The theme of the Book of Romans is the gospel of Christ. Paul was not ashamed of this gospel because he knew it was the answer to man's great need. Adam's sin had plunged the whole world into spiritual darkness. All are spiritually dead without Christ. The gospel of which Paul was not ashamed was the Good News that Christ makes alive spiritually all who receive Him as Saviour. When a person receives Christ as Saviour, the righteousness of God is imputed to him. Thus, man becomes justified—declared righteous before God.

Sin

Although God is a God of love, He is also righteous and expresses His wrath against sin. God could not be God if He loved evil. God's wrath is against all ungodliness—against all who live without God. God's wrath is contemporary—it is expressed at the present as well as in the past and in the future. God's wrath is all inclusive—it is against all evil. God's wrath is absolutely inescapable—no unsaved person will be free from it. And God's wrath is justifiable—man deserves his punishment because he refuses God's love.

God has revealed Himself to all men so that all are without excuse. Romans 1:19,20 records that God has revealed Himself through nature—"the things that are made." This revelation through nature is adequate to show man that God exists and that He is the Creator, Designer and Provider for His universe. However, the personal revelation of God in redemption is seen only in Christ and is revealed through the Bible—God's written revelation.

When man refuses to turn his life over to God he becomes all the more engulfed by sin. Romans 1:21-23 reveals sin's progression in the life of the unsaved person. First, man simply refuses to acknowledge God—"they glorified him not as God." Second, man's attitude becomes one of ingratitude—"neither were thankful." Third, man's speculation about God becomes futile—"but became vain in their imaginations." When sin progresses this far in the unsaved person's heart his moral choices are of the wrong kind—"their foolish heart was darkened."

Sin has its consequences. It is a law or principle of spiritual harvest that "whatsoever a man soweth, that shall he also reap" (Gal. 6:7). God will not force men to worship Him. But when men choose to forsake God and worship the creature rather than the Creator, then God gives them over to the control of the sinful things they prefer—besides eternal condemnation at the end of their earthly lives. Three times in the closing portion of Romans 1 is the expression: "God gave them up" (vv. 24,26,28). The final verse of the chapter shows that such persons are confirmed in their own unholiness.

But as black as this picture is, God has a remedy for each person who will turn to Him seeking forgiveness through Jesus Christ. No wonder Paul was not ashamed of the gospel of Christ. It takes sinners such as are described in Romans 1 and makes them fit to stand before God.

The moralist of Romans 2 is one who judges another on the basis of his own moral standards. He does not know God's righteousness and condemnation of all men as sinners. God's answer to the moralist is that he also faces the same condemnation as the person whom he despises. Since we are all sinners by birth it is not a question of how good we are in our own eyes —everyone needs to receive Christ to escape sin's condemnation.

God's Judgment

God's judgment on sin is righteous and justifiable, for His judgment is based on man's deeds. However, man is never saved by his works, because salvation is only by grace through faith in Christ (Eph. 2:8,9). But whereas the Christian is judged according to the deeds he had done for Christ, the unsaved person is judged according to the deeds he has done for unrighteousness.

God also judges according to the light a person has received. There is a difference in the amount of light different people have, yet all have sufficient light so that they know God exists and that they have come short of His glory.

Man is also to be judged according to the gospel—that Christ died for sinners, that He was buried and rose again (I Cor. 15:1-4).

The Israelites had much light revealed to them, for it was to this nation that God gave His written revelation. They, of all people, should have welcomed the arrival of the Messiah, but they rejected and crucified Him. The Jews were proud of their religious ceremonies but their hearts were not right before God. Even though the nation Israel rejected God, He remains faithful and will someday yet fulfill His promises to the Jewish nation. But God will not work with the nation Israel again until His purpose is accomplished for and through the Church, the Body of Christ.

During every age mankind has been in a state of spiritual corruption—"all have sinned and come short of the glory of God" (Rom. 3:23). No one is able, of himself, to produce the righteousness which God requires. Man's tongue expresses what is in his heart and the tongue is pictured by the Scriptures as a world of iniquity because this is what man's heart is like. And since his heart is wicked, man's feet are "swift to shed blood" (Rom. 3:15). Man's basic problem is that he does not fear God.

The Law

Since Adam's time man has been a sinner but not all people were conscious of the fact that the things they did were in disobedience to God. For this reason God gave the law which reflects His holy character. The law does not bring salvation to any person—only condemnation. The law was given that it might be a moral mirror to reflect God's holiness. Romans 3 tells of the purpose of the law—to give knowledge of sin so that all might be without excuse before God.

God did not give the law so that men would try to live up to it in order to receive salvation. The law was given to show man God's holiness so that all mankind would realize how far short they had come of God's glory and that it would be impossible to live up to such standards in their own ability. The law was to show man his failure and inability to keep the standards of God so that he would turn to God in faith to receive salvation. Salvation has always been by faith in every age although the rule of life for the believer has varied.

Since the law cannot save it is necessary for God to have a method of redemption. And what we could not do, Christ did. He himself fully met every demand of the law. Christ fulfilled all righteousness.

God is holy and cannot approve of sin. But His Son Jesus Christ died in our place and paid the penalty for our sin—thus satisfying the Heavenly Father for our sin. Therefore, God was able to provide redemption without lowering His standards against evil. When we receive Christ as Saviour His righteousness is imputed or placed on our account. Christ not only forgives our sin, He gives life to us which lasts forever. This act of God not only frees us from the guilt of sin but also from the power of sin.

Right Standing With God

How a person may obtain a right standing with God is clearly illustrated in the life of Abraham. He believed God and this act of faith was "counted to him for righteousness" (Rom. 4:3).

The Scriptures present two aspects of being justified. Paul speaks of that which justifies a man before God—that of faith in God which is taking God at His Word. James emphasizes the proof of justification—that of good works which result from true faith. Justifying faith is the faith which receives Christ as Saviour, merely to believe that God exists is not saving faith. One must personally receive Christ in order to be delivered from condemnation.

There are many results of justification and several of these are presented in Romans 5. There is peace with God for the person who has received Christ as Saviour. An entrance or access into the grace of God is another result of justification. Our relationship with God through Christ is such that we may enter His presence at any time. The believer also senses the presence of God in his daily life. No matter what the circumstances Christ has promised that He will never leave or forsake the Christian.

Because the believer has his heart fixed on that which is eternal rather than that which is temporal he is able to endure trials with the right attitude. He knows that God is working all things together for his good even though he may not understand the trials of the present. Another characteristic of the justified person is that the love of God is expressed through his life. This is a love so great that it loves the unlovely—this love originates only with God. God also promises to save His children from wrath because the Christian is delivered from all condemnation.

Sin gained its entrance into the world through the man, Adam. Death is a result of sin and the fact that all die proves that sin has passed upon all. There is a distinction between a sin nature and acts of sin. It is because a person has a sin nature that he commits acts of sin. Through the offence of Adam came death, but through the grace of Jesus Christ salvation is provided for every person.

The first five chapters of Romans show that salvation is needed by every person and has been provided through Christ. The basis of the victorious life is also seen in that Christ has not only delivered us from the guilt of sin but also from the power of sin. Through Christ has come the "abundance of grace" (Rom. 5:17).

Memory Assignment:
Memorize Romans 5:21.

EXAMINATION

Complete the following:

1. The theme of the Book of Romans is the _____ _____ _____.

2. When a person receives Christ as Saviour, he is declared _____ before God.

3. When a person refuses to turn his life over to God he becomes all the more engulfed by _____.

4. Romans 1:21-28 illustrates the principle of spiritual harvest: "Whatsoever a man _____, that shall he also _____."

5. God's judgment on sin is righteous and justifiable because it is based on man's _____.

In the right-hand margin write "True" or "False" after each of the following statements:

6. God judges according to the light a person has received.
   _____

7. Man will be judged according to the gospel. _____

8. During every age man has been in a state of spiritual corruption. _____

9. The purpose of the law is to give knowledge of sin so that all might be without excuse before God. _____

10. God gave the law so men would try to live up to it in order to receive salvation. _____

In the blank space at the right-hand margin write the letter of the correct or most nearly correct answer.

11. Salvation has been through faith:
    (a) only since Christ died for our sins
    (b) before Moses gave the law and after Christ's death only
    (c) in every age _____

12. When we receive Christ as Saviour:
    (a) His righteousness is placed on our account
    (b) we are then free to live as we wish
    (c) we are then in a position to please God by keeping His law _____

13. Romans 4 tells how the life of Abraham illustrates:
    (a) that religious ceremonies contribute to our salvation
    (b) that keeping the law is necessary for salvation
    (c) that a believer's faith is counted to him for righteousness _____

14. While Paul emphasizes that justification is by faith, James emphasizes:
    (a) that justification is by works of the law
    (b) that works are the proof of justifying faith
    (c) that works are not related to faith _____

15. Romans 1-5 teaches that every person needs salvation and that:
    (a) all will be saved
    (b) Christ has provided salvation for all
    (c) those who live up to the law will be saved _____

☐ **I have memorized Romans 5:21.**

ANSWER KEY

After completing each examination, check your answers with these. Check memory verses in your Bible.

UNIT 1
1. Jesus.
2. Christ.
3. Lord.
4. Grace.
5. Power, God, salvation.
6. c.
7. b.
8. b.
9. c.
10. a or b.
11. False.
12. False.
13. False.
14. True.
15. True.

UNIT 2
1. True.
2. False.
3. False.
4. True.
5. False.
6. b.
7. c.
8. b.
9. a.
10. a.
11. Inescapable.
12. Revelation or knowledge.
13. Cause, effect.
14. Without excuse.
15. Christ, Bible.

UNIT 3
1. Impiety.
2. Thankful.
3. Reason.
4. Fools.
5. Image, man.
6. False.
7. False.
8. True.
9. True.
10. False.
11. c.
12. c.
13. a.
14. b.
15. c.

UNIT 4
1. False.
2. False.
3. False.
4. False.
5. True.
6. Kindness or longsuffering.
7. Deeds.
8. Respect.
9. Light, gospel (of Jesus Christ).
10. Conduct.
11. c.
12. b.
13. a.
14. b.
15. c.

UNIT 5
1. c.
2. b.
3. c.
4. b.
5. c.
6. Failed.
7. Inwardly.
8. Life.
9. Word.
10. Gentiles.
11. False.
12. False.
13. True.
14. False.
15. True.

UNIT 6
1. Spiritual.
2. Sinned, short.
3. None, not one.
4. God's.
5. God.
6. c.
7. a.
8. c.
9. a.
10. b.
11. True.
12. False.
13. False.
14. True.
15. False.

UNIT 7
1. No flesh.
2. God.
3. Lost.
4. Excuse.
5. God.
6. b.
7. b.
8. b.

100

9. c.
10. a.
11. True.
12. True.
13. False.
14. True.
15. True.

UNIT 8
1. True.
2. False.
3. True.
4. True.
5. False.
6. Unchanged.
7. Grace.
8. Sinned.
9. Death.
10. Died.
11. c.
12. b.
13. c.
14. b.
15. b.

UNIT 9
1. c.
2. a.
3. b.
4. b.
5. c.
6. False.
7. False.
8. True.
9. False.
10. False.
11. Before.
12. Before.
13. Faith, grace.
14. Death, resurrection.
15. Resurrection.

UNIT 10
1. Peace.
2. Access.
3. Grace.
4. Leave, forsake.
5. Glory.
6. True.
7. True.
8. False.
9. True.
10. False.
11. c.
12. b.
13. a.
14. b.
15. b.

UNIT 11
1. Adam, Christ.
2. All.
3. Nature, acts.
4. Death.
5. Law.
6. a.
7. c.
8. b.
9. c.
10. b.
11. False.
12. False.
13. False.
14. True.
15. True.

UNIT 12
1. Gospel of Christ.
2. Righteous.
3. Sin.
4. Soweth, reap.
5. Deeds.
6. True.
7. True.

8. True.
9. True.
10. False.
11. c.
12. a.
13. c.
14. b.
15. b.